Progress: A Christian Doctrine?

A. G. B. WOOLLARD

Progress: A Christian Doctrine?

LONDON

S·P·C·K

1972

First published in 1972
by S.P.C.K.
Holy Trinity Church
Marylebone Road
London, N.W.1.

Printed in Great Britain by
The Camelot Press Ltd, London and Southampton

SBN 281 02665

Contents

Introduction

Can Christians affirm faith in human progress?

For most Christian traditions, during a great deal of Christian history, the answer has been "no". There has been a widespread tendency to devalue "this world" in favour of the "other world"; and this negative attitude to the present life was only to be expected at a time when that life was "nasty, brutish, and short" and showed no signs of changing. Some traditions (Troeltsch's "Church type")[1] affirmed, and indeed consecrated, the existing order of society as the arena of man's sanctification and preparation for heaven; others (most, though not all, of the "sects") were indifferent or antagonistic to the existing culture, but withdrew from it rather than seeking to change it. Only one tradition— the Augustinian-Calvinist, whose faith, as Richard Niebuhr put it,[2] is in "Christ the Transformer of Culture"—has shown very much explicit concern for progress from a Christian viewpoint; and this most notably in its American form,[3] and more particularly in the nineteenth and twentieth centuries as the possibility of real and rapid social change impressed itself upon Western culture.

In order to consider the possibility of a contemporary Christian doctrine of progress, therefore, we must begin with the way in which this doctrine evolved in American Protestantism—particularly in the movement known as the "Social Gospel", which had its parallels both in Britain and in Europe, but must be examined in its American form in order to find its purest essence. If we are to relate this stage of thought adequately to contemporary problems, however, we must view the Social Gospel as it were over

[1] E. Troeltsch, *The Social Teaching of the Christian Churches*
[2] H. R. Niebuhr, *Christ and Culture*. cf. in the present context R. Preston, "Christians and Economic Growth", in D. L. Menby (ed.) *Economic Growth in World Perspective*
[3] cf. H. R. Niebuhr, *The Kingdom of God in America*

the shoulder of that theological giant who is at once its most
notable son and its most trenchant critic, and who has done
more than anyone else to formulate contemporary Christian
attitudes to history and to social, political, and economic issues.
I refer, of course, to Reinhold Niebuhr.

We must look closely at Niebuhr's basic presuppositions in the
light of the cultural ethos which predominated during the post-
1914 period during which he wrote his major works. Then we
must examine the way in which these presuppositions were trans-
muted by other theologians in the different cultural atmosphere
of the 1950s and early 1960s. And finally we must ask what new
factors in our own time—a time of many growing crises—pose
basic challenges to this whole tradition of Christian thought about
progress, and how this might affect a truly contemporary doctrine
of progress.

For we must never neglect the cultural backcloth of Christian
theology. During the period under review secular ideas of progress
have undergone quite considerable changes. From a strong
optimism at the turn of the century the Western world moved,
as we shall see, into a phase of deep pessimism in the inter-war
years; then, after the Second World War, to a strange new kind
of optimism and perhaps, more recently still, to a new and complex
pessimism. All these changes have had their effect on theological
thought and the Christian understanding of history and social
change. The very meaning of the word "progress", as well as
our attitudes to it, has been far from static.

If we assume that social change has a part in God's purposes,
is it to be achieved by man alone, by God alone, or by the two
working in co-operation? And what exactly is the "cash value" of
these three possibilities? What difference does it make in practice
if one of them is true and the others false? Further, how much
social change is possible? What is the appropriate Christian
"style of life" in a time of change? and can the change which we
desire, and must work for, be summed up in some neat formula,
or is it highly complex or even indefinable? I hope that answers to
some of these questions—or at least hints towards answers—
will emerge in the following discussions.

It would of course be wrong rigidly to limit such a discussion
to American Reformed theology. This indeed provides the context
in which most of the important ideas have germinated, but it

will be necessary from time to time to refer to developments in Anglicanism, Continental Protestantism, and (increasingly in our time) Roman Catholicism. However, we will weave our story around the "Apostolic Succession" of American Protestant thinkers about progress: the Social Gospellers, Reinhold Niebuhr, Harvey Cox, and the process-theologians. The background to the debate may now be shifting from America to Europe and even (as we shall see) to Asia and other parts of the "third world"; we shall have reason to question whether American culture can any longer supply the needed material for the debate. But just as America herself has for two centuries played a key role in the human hope of material and social progress, so the contribution of American theologians to the "debate about progress" has been a central and vital one, for which the whole Church will always be in their debt.

1

From
Optimism to Pessimism:
The Social Gospel and the
First World War

The late nineteenth and early twentieth centuries were a time of great optimism in the Western world. The results of the Industrial Revolution and of the political revolution—the emancipation of the new middle classes, which in so many lands followed hard upon it—had suggested that real advances in human well-being were possible. Nowhere was this clearer than in America, the "land of the free", built on a doctrine of individual freedom and enterprise under which humble people could exploit the vast natural resources of an almost virgin continent and—if only they were energetic enough—could win for themselves a wealth and a power which would have been impossible in feudal Europe.

At the same time the enormous human cost of the Industrial Revolution was being recognized, and many forces—from Evangelical philanthropy to militant Marxism—were mobilized to mitigate it. If there had been casualties in the onward march of progress there seemed no reason why they should not be enabled to take their rightful place, with a little help, in the new, free, and prosperous society. Along with material progress, gradually but steadily catching up with it, there seemed to be a progress of human conscience, an emerging awareness of the "brotherhood of man".

It was not surprising under such circumstances that the new idea of evolution of the natural order, crystallized and popularized by the discoveries and hypotheses of Darwin, should be applied to the human order as well. Man and society were evolving, not now on a biological but on a sociological plane.[1] It was natural that many Christians should feel that they needed to come to terms with this new world view of science, and indeed to trace in it the hand of God.

Against this background, then, evolved the theology of the Social Gospel. Whilst there were considerable differences between the protagonists of this school—men such as Washington Gladden, Shailer Mathews, and Walter Rauschenbusch—they held certain central convictions in common. Let us examine some of these in detail.

Our generation has been brought up to view the Social Gospel through the eyes of Richard Niebuhr: "A God without wrath brought men without sin into a Kingdom without judgement, through the ministration of a Christ without a Cross."[2] The picture is one of a theology which turned the Christian faith into a simple, this-worldly ethical system and saw the Kingdom coming as a result of a few not very costly revisions of the social order. This is unfair. Rauschenbusch, for one, had a profound awareness of sin, and of God's judgement addressed to the whole of American society. He it was who wrote vividly of the "Kingdom of Evil" against which the protagonists of God's Kingdom had to fight.[3] Both he and other leaders of the movement such as Richard Ely[4] were well aware of the cost of discipleship. The price of winning the Kingdom was not cheap.

Nor is it true either that they believed that evolution would bring the Kingdom automatically, or that social reform would do away with sin. Rauschenbusch in particular saw that sin is endemic even in the best social order,[5] and Daniel Day Williams cites another leader of the movement, H. E. Fosdick, as denying that the universe is "fool-proof" or "automatically progressive".[6] And it is most certainly not true that they thought that man could

[1] For a discussion of "Social Darwinism" see F. W. Matson, *The Broken Image*, pp. 36-45. This excellent work is a discussion of science's image of man as it has evolved over the past century, and the passage cited should be read against the background of the whole book. For a good description of the theological response to Darwin, see I. G. Barbour, *Issues in Science and Religion*, pp. 98-110

[2] Niebuhr, *The Kingdom of God in America*, p. 193

[3] cf. the passage in *The Social Gospel in America*, ed. Hardy, pp. 378-89

[4] "The Social Law of Service", Handy, op. cit., pp. 221-34

[5] Handy, op. cit., p. 340

[6] Williams, *God's Grace and Man's Hope*, p. 26

achieve the Kingdom simply by his own efforts. Rauschenbusch insisted that the Kingdom is "miraculous all the way";[1] the role of God is central, and with him man can but co-operate.

Yet there were certain new, and some would say totally un-biblical, presuppositions in their thought. They followed the liberal theologians of Europe, notably Ritschl and Harnack, in their suspicion of metaphysics and super-naturalism; and so, in their desire to relate the Christian faith to the world view of their time, they sought to reduce it to what would have "cash-value" in terms of the empirical scientific method.[2] This led to a view of religion (following Ritschl) purely in terms of its social and ethical value; as an affirmation of man's true exalted place in the scheme of things, and a set of moral guidelines for the evolution of society towards the Kingdom. The Christian faith was reduced, in Harnack's famous phrase, to "the Fatherhood of God and the Brotherhood of Man"; and those aspects of traditional doctrine which could not be fitted easily into this image tended to be drastically reinterpreted or discarded.

Beach and Niebuhr, in their commentary on the evolution of Christian ethics, sum up the basic theme of the Social Gospel as "the stress on the principle of continuity in the cosmos . . . rather than jumps and chasms and dualisms, which are more typical of the biblical world view and of much traditional the-ology".[3] Among other things, this involved an insistence on the continuity between God and man; and hence the "democratiza-tion" of God, an idea on which all the Social Gospel leaders place much emphasis, and which is perhaps most fully worked out in Gladden's lecture on the Incarnation.[4] God is now seen as man's co-worker rather than his sovereign Lord—an idea suited, both to those passages in the Gospels which speak of intimacy with the heavenly Father and also to democratic American culture. This does *not* mean that the awareness of God as transcendent Judge

[1] W. Beach and H. R. Niebuhr (eds.), *Christian Ethics*, p. 469

[2] On the scientific world-view of the period see Barbour, op. cit., ch. 4. He notes the difference between those philosophies and theologies which fitted man neatly into the Darwinian naturalistic scheme, and those (the majority) which, influenced by idealism, carved out for man and his religion a special place in the new world. Elements of both appeared in the Social Gospel; both, as we shall see, have proved unable to come to terms with the more complex world-view of more recent science

[3] Beach and Niebuhr, op. cit., p. 450

[4] Handy, op. cit., pp. 154–69

was lost; but it was perhaps eclipsed by the preaching of the immanent Colleague. This undoubtedly led to a temptation to picture God in the image of a turn-of-the-century American liberal. Jean Russell, in her indictment of the Social Gospel for failing to get to grips with the racial issue,[1] suggests that this is why white American self-understanding could not be challenged at the very point where it most needed an external standard.

This emphasis on continuity also led some thinkers—notably Gladden[2]—to emphasize both the desirability and the possibility of solving industrial and other social problems by co-operation rather than conflict. In its popularized form the Social Gospel tended to assume that if only all men acted as brothers, everything would be all right; and they *would* act as brothers once they were convinced of the reality of the "Brotherhood of Man". Most of the leaders—Rauschenbusch was perhaps an exception here— therefore had a deep suspicion of socialism with its stress on class warfare and its assumption that the bourgeoisie would give up its privileges only if coerced. Better, thought the Social Gospellers, to preach to the ruling classes the ideal of "service"[3] and hope that enlightened men would respond.

This affirmation of continuity as almost a basic metaphysical principle would seem to have a third implication, though it is nowhere, as far as I know, spelled out. This is that evolution proceeds in a straight line; that progress is a simple and not a complex conception. In his discussion of the relationship between the theology of Harvey Cox and that of the Social Gospel,[4] David Little suggests that Rauschenbusch and his fellows set up certain principles—democracy, freedom, solidarity—as absolutes and thought that the single-hearted pursuit of them would bring progress; and this absolutism, this consecration of specific human values in the name of the Kingdom, was a major target for their neo-orthodox critics. Be that as it may, the Social Gospellers

[1] Russell, *God's Lost Cause*, pp. 87f. We shall be returning to this topic as one of the points with which all recent theological discussions of progress have failed adequately to deal

[2] "Is it peace or war?", Handy, op. cit., pp. 49–72

[3] For a brilliant satire of the American bourgeois ideal of service Sinclair Lewis' famous novel *Babbitt* should be read. An intelligent left-wing critique of this ideal may be found in R. Williams, *Culture and Society, 1780–1950*, pp. 314–18

[4] D. Little, "The Social Gospel Revisited", in D. Callahan (ed.), *The Secular City Debate*

seemed to have a fairly clear idea, and a remarkably confident belief, that social evolution should go (for some, *was* going) in one particular direction, and that an extrapolation along this line would eventually lead to the Kingdom. It is true that for most of them this direction was that of social solidarity rather than the individualistic survival-of-the-fittest to which mainstream Social Darwinism, and contemporary American society, gave its blessing.[1] Most of them, however, stopped short of an unAmerican socialism and seemed to assume that, if American democracy in its existing form developed to its logical conclusion, its current inadequacies would be ironed out and the Kingdom would be achieved.[2]

This last presupposition—the hope placed in American-style democracy—was, I suggest, the greatest weakness of the Social Gospellers. For though indeed they criticized many aspects of the *status quo*, they were confident that this *could* evolve into the Kingdom. The idea that genuine progress might require a radically new turn—might even involve the total condemnation of the existing culture—never seemed to occur to them; still less did they have the resources for working out what this radical change might entail and how Christians could co-operate in bringing it about. Hence they could never shake themselves free from certain aspects of the American ideology—notably the antagonism to socialistic models of society. Hence also they were tempted to see, in the hegemony of the white race, the beneficent result of the evolutionary process, understood in Darwinian terms.[3] And hence they were unprepared for the cultural crisis which befell the Western world in 1914.

In 1912, Rauschenbusch could write, "The largest and hardest part of the work of Christianizing the social order has been done".[4] Two years later, the forces of evil were unleashed on a scale never before known to man.

[1] But cf. Matson, loc. cit., for the complex nature of Social Darwinism. And it must be remembered that liberal theology was essentially idealistic—asserting the primacy of man over nature—rather than naturalistic, so that, whilst in accord with the thought of the time it expressed fairly simplistic evolutionary doctrines of society, it was not tied down to Darwinian formulae

[2] cf. especially Gladden, "The Nation and the Kingdom", Handy, op. cit., pp. 135–53

[3] cf. Russell, loc. cit   [4] Handy, op. cit., p. 339

The shock which the First World War delivered to Western culture was, to be sure, a delayed one. It needed the collapse of the economic system in the 1930s, and the growing realization that that one dreadful holocaust was not after all destined to be "the war to end all wars", before many became convinced of the fundamental sickness of society and the harbingers of progress found themselves "hollow men" in a "waste land".[1] But it was not very long before philosophers and theologians began to preach a withdrawal from this decaying society, a negation of all hopes of progress, and a search for a more enduring reality, whether in the Transcendent or in the inner self.

Karl Barth, Rudolf Bultmann, and Paul Tillich, the three very different prophets of "neo-orthodox" Christianity, were all of them very much products of the First World War. Their characteristic "No" to the culture-Christianity of liberalism does not date from before 1914; indeed Barth and Tillich had been reared in the tradition of liberal social theology associated on the Continent with Blumhardt, Kutter, and Ragaz. Whilst Tillich never completely severed his links with German religious socialism, and whilst (as we shall see) a real social concern remained even in Barth, they were both profoundly "converted" by their wartime experiences. For Bultmann likewise a cultural pessimism induced by the war joined hands with a deep awareness of the threat to traditional Christianity posed by the empirical scientific method, to produce an existentialist theology in which faith became wholly a matter of self-understanding—man called out of sin and death to "authentic existence" by a wholly transcendent God; a God whose presence could not be seen at all in external things, in society, or culture, so that all language which located him there had to be "demythologized" to find its true, inward meaning.

Neither Barth nor Tillich was totally happy with Bultmann's expression of the Gospel. For Barth, God was the "wholly Other", who could not be expressed in terms of human self-understanding any more than he could in terms of culture. Tillich took culture much more seriously, demanding that the Church listen to the questions that the world was asking; this included a concern, which he shared with Bultmann and other existentialists, for the insights of depth-psychology as they reveal to the theologian the

[1] T. S. Eliot's romantic harking back to the past may have been an extreme reaction to the social crisis; but it was not entirely untypical

nature and extent of the existential crisis of contemporary man. But unlike both Bultmann and Barth, he sought to press on through human self-understanding to a new metaphysic (or, as he would prefer to call it, a new ontology) and to base a world view on the idea of God as "Being-itself", rather than merely speaking, in a non-metaphysical and transcendental way, about man's encounter with the Word. For all their differences, however, these three men tended to see the Christian primarily, if not exclusively, as one standing before God in his subjectivity and thus experiencing judgement and grace; not as one seeking God and his Kingdom in the struggle for social progress.

I do not intend to discuss in detail the attitudes to progress which these three men held; it has been discussed adequately elsewhere.[1] Suffice it to say that all three sought the ultimate reality, the Kingdom, more or less outside history. For Barth the Kingdom is Christ himself, the incarnation of the wholly Other within history; history is thus only interesting in so far as there is (to use a term dear to some of Barth's later followers) such a thing as "salvation history", in which Creation, the Old Covenant, the Incarnation and Atonement, the time of the Church, and the End all have their place (more or less independently of secular history) and through which we are linked to the One who transcends history. For Bultmann the Kingdom is the life of "authentic existence", the response of faith in the immediate present to which past and future are irrelevant. For Tillich it is "participation in the New Being", which breaks into history at certain moments (*kairoi*) and is defined by the central historical event of the Incarnation, but which, because of Tillich's Platonizing tendencies, tends to be basically a-historical.[2]

---

[1] For Barth and Bultmann in particular see J. Moltmann, *Theology of Hope*, especially ch. 1. This book is an important critique of recent Continental Protestant theology for its lack of vision of the future; it deserves more attention than I can give it here, but its author, despite brave attempts, never really breaks out of the theological tradition which he is criticizing and ends up with an "eschatology" hardly more sophisticated than that of the American "secular theology" which we shall be discussing later. For case studies of Barth's and Tillich's contribution on a particular issue see C. C. West, *Communism and the Theologians*

[2] Tillich was indeed concerned about history, and in particular his discussion of the ambiguities of history in the final section of his *Systematic Theology* is profound. But his wisdom is marred by his suspicion of utopianism; his seeming uncertainty about the "cash value" (other than existential) of eschatological hope; and his general tendency to look *through* outward things as "symbols"

None of the great neo-orthodox theologians, then, really comes to grips with history. Bultmann, to be sure, is interested in "historicality", the "time-ful" nature of man's existence,[1] but this is a matter of individual experience not of concrete events, and outward history remains irrelevant. And this is perhaps why he and his followers had no resources wherewith to criticize the Hitler régime, and were mostly to be found on the side of the "German Christians" in the great division of the German Church in 1934. But it was just at this point that Barth[2] did have something to say and made his major contribution to contemporary Christian thought about progress.

For the great theme of neo-orthodoxy is the distance between God the judge and man the sinner. The one thing that a Barthian cannot tolerate in the social realm is the spectacle of man setting himself up in the place of God and claiming absolute dominion. If man is finite and utterly sinful all social and political absolutism must be condemned. And the German Church struggle was essentially a repudiation of Hitler's claim to absolute dominion even over the Church and religion of the German people.

The great Barmen Declaration of 1934, in which the "Confessing Church" claimed Christ as the one Lord of heaven and earth and in his name rejected Hitler's demand for subservience, was largely inspired by Barth. In this act neo-orthodoxy revealed its one social principle; all human claims and achievements, all authorities, all ideals, are *relative*. Social and political absolutisms stand condemned. And by implication the ideal society is one in which absolute claims for any power or ideology—even for the Church—are cut down to size by the political structure and the social ethos; in short, what was later to be called a "secular" society.

[1] This concept, derived from Heidegger, is developed by Gogarten. cf. Moltmann, op. cit., pp. 311–16, and L. Shiner, *The Secularization of History, an introduction to the theology of Friedrich Gogarten*, especially ch. 2

[2] The more politically active Tillich had already been exiled to the U.S.A. He does not seem to have been involved in social issues there

of the "depth" which is the "really real", based on an almost Platonic division between the realms of essence and existence. cf. J. L. Adams, "Tillich's Interpretation of History", in C. W. Kegley and R. W. Bretall (eds.) *The Theology of Paul Tillich* and the pertinent questions addressed to Tillich at the end of that essay

This idea—that social progress is under judgement and that the category of human sin, rather than that of human achievement, is the key to the interpretation of history and demands a rejection of all utopianism—was taken up by a young pastor from industrial Detroit named Reinhold Niebuhr. The theological and ethical construction which he built on this foundation is undoubtedly the greatest individual contribution to Christian social thinking so far this century and we must now examine it in some detail.

2

The Legacy of Reinhold Niebuhr

In order to assess the contribution of Niebuhr to the contemporary debate about progress I do not intend to go into excessive detail about the development of his thought or its relevance to specific issues,[1] nor do I propose to give a full account of the background of his political involvement out of which that thought emerged.[2] It is necessary merely to depict this man, his life and thought, in bold outline, and to ask in general terms about his influence on Christian social thinking and its implications for our problem of progress.

The disillusionment with liberal optimism, which for Barth and his fellows had emerged from the arena of war, came for Niebuhr in the situation of a pastorate in industrial Detroit, at the time of the building up of the motor industry there and the first attempts to organize its workers.[3] His experience of the terrible insecurity of the working classes, their lack of freedom in that "land of the free", drove him to a deep sympathy with the Marxist interpretation of history as a class-struggle in which justice can only be achieved at great cost, not by a smooth social evolution.

His first major work, *Moral Man and Immoral Society*, is a brilliant exposition of the corporate human will-to-power and its corruptions, drawing at once on the Marxist concept of ideology and the Christian doctrine of original sin. His conviction that original sin is the most manifest and powerful force in human history is expounded in all his writings from that time onwards and is perhaps his major theoretical contribution to Christian social ethics. Briefly we may outline his thesis thus: individual men are indeed capable of self-sacrifice and altruism, but this is

[1] cf. C. W. Kegley and R. W. Bretall (eds.), *Reinhold Niebuhr, His Political, Social and Religious Thought*

[2] cf. D. Meyer, *The Protestant Search for Political Realism*

[3] This period of his life, before he moved to an academic career, is well documented in his *Leaves from the Notebook of a Tamed Cynic*

largely and unconsciously channelled towards evil corporate ends, of which inordinate patriotism is an obvious example. It is thus possible for man to be very "moral" and self-giving in the service of an "immoral" group selfishness. Now since (it would seem) only individuals can be unselfish, and groups cannot, all individual self-sacrifice is likely to be mis-channelled in this way towards the selfish advantage of some group.[1] Thus altruism and idealism would seem to be irrelevant on the social plane; the only power that operates at this level of human existence is the clash of group self-interests.

At the same time, Niebuhr observes, political man is not "totally depraved". For he sees the need to "rationalize" the self-interest of the group, to identify it with an ideal; a war, for example, may be justified by the "need to defend democracy". If our politicians in all their Machiavellianism had no conscience, no spark of light, no idealism and no shame—if these did not exist, indeed, at group as well as individual levels—such rationalization would not seem necessary and power could be used nakedly. The existence of human conscience, the pursuit of reason, and the aspirations of religion—all these are real goods operating on the plane of history. Yet they are two-edged swords, for, especially in the hands of nations and groups, religious and rational ideals can be used as a cloak for sheer self-interest and as a sanctification for terrible outrages.[2]

This image of man as sinner and its relevance in historical interpretation is expounded fully in Niebuhr's famous Gifford lectures, *The Nature and Destiny of Man*. Here sin is shown to be a concomitant of man's anxiety—his exposed position in the universe, in the face of his own finitude, to which he responds either by grasping what little control he can over nature and his neighbours in a pathetic imitation of God (pride), or by fleeing the pain of human self-awareness and taking refuge in an "animal" style of life (sensuality).[3] Thus, by failing to accept his finitude and trust in the infinite God, man is doomed to corruption. Niebuhr emphasizes once more that this depravity is not total, for man is aware of moral issues, he feels the judgement of his conscience, and he can aspire to religious and rational greatness; and yet again the depravity *is* in a sense total, for these very

[1] *Moral Man and Immoral Society*, ch. 2 and *passim*
[2] ibid., ch. 5   [3] *Nature and Destiny of Man*, Vol. I, chs. 6–8

aspirations and potentialities of man become the most powerful vehicles of hypocrisy and evil.

The first implication of Niebuhr's strongly Pauline emphasis on human sin is a rejection of the liberal hope that the growth of reason and of an enlightened corporate conscience will usher in the age of brotherhood. For these very qualities of human life—most notably reason, and man's rational control over his environment, which does indeed develop over time—are the most powerful tools of evil for man's corrupt will.[1] In the collapse of the *laissez-faire* economic system in the 1930s, and the parallel rise of a sophisticated régime of evil in Germany, Niebuhr saw his rejection of liberal optimism vindicated.

The next result of this emphasis on the permanence of sin is a challenge to the naïve attempt of those (including many Social Gospellers) who sought to "apply the teachings of Jesus" directly to questions of social justice. In his *Interpretation of Christian Ethics*, and later in Volume II of *The Nature and Destiny of Man*, Niebuhr shows how the Christian ideal of sacrificial love is an "impossible possibility" within social and political history. The behaviour of classes and nations is dictated by self-interest; this may indeed rise to the level of a sort of mutual love, a *quid pro quo* in which, in their own interests, men and nations agree on some sort of mutual security and the maintenance of a certain level of justice. Real Christian love, *agape*, is not directly relevant here; the preaching of high ideals only gives a new opportunity for sanctifying self-interest in the name of those ideals. And Niebuhr has no difficulty in showing how the quest for a "Christian" solution to social injustices—the way of peace and conciliation—can lead to a sanctification of the *status quo* by the middle classes who have most to lose by any more violent attempts to right the wrong.[2]

Yet *agape* is not entirely irrelevant in history. The fact that Christ's love led him to the Cross shows that the way of self-giving cannot hope for worldly success in the way that the Social Gospellers believed; yet, says Niebuhr, new ventures in brotherhood and justice can only be initiated by daring acts of sacrificial love which look for no *quid pro quo*. In one of his most "optimistic" passages he writes:

[1] cf. *Nature and Destiny of Man*, Vol. I, ch. 4; *Faith and History*, chs. 5–6
[2] cf. *Moral Man and Immoral Society*, ch. 5; *An Interpretation of Christian Ethics*, ch. 6; *Nature and Destiny of Man*, Vol. II, ch. 3

> There are no limits to be set in history for the achievements
> of universal brotherhood . . . the *agape* of the Kingdom of God
> [is] a resource for infinite developments towards more perfect
> brotherhood.[1]

In radically challenging all existing, and indeed all possible,
social orders and showing up the rough justice and self-interest
which underlies them, Christian love can draw them onward to
higher levels indefinitely.

What are the conclusions for Christian social and political action
which Niebuhr draws from all this? They can be summed up in
the famous phrase "Christian Realism". The Christian ideal of
sacrificial love though a perpetual challenge cannot be fully
realized on the plane of history; therefore Christians must seek
for a tolerable justice, in which men's ineradicable self-interest is
harnessed for the universal good. This will evidently mean some
compromise of those "Christian principles" which certain liberals
tried to derive directly from the Sermon on the Mount; in particular it may mean involvement in conflict, with all its moral
ambiguities, for the sake of bringing justice to the oppressed.
Pacifism, though it may seem the "ideal" stance for a Christian
to take in the struggle between classes and nations, may be a
positive evil if, by discouraging participation in the fight for
change, it helps to buttress up an unjust *status quo*.[2]

What, then, is the kind of society towards which Christians
should work? If there is and can be progress (we shall shortly
discuss Niebuhr's position on this in more detail), which way
should it go? Here we can detect an interesting shift in Niebuhr's
thinking over the years, in which the strengths and weaknesses
of his basic presuppositions are clearly illustrated.[3]

In his early days, as we have seen, Niebuhr was deeply sympathetic to Marxism. He was attracted in particular by the Marxist
claim that the bourgeois ideal of peace in society and of a gentle,
evolutionary progress was a product of the self-interest of those
who benefited from such a state of affairs. He was attracted by the
"realism" of a passion for justice which admitted the bitter fact

[1] *Nature and Destiny of Man*, Vol. II, p. 85

[2] Niebuhr would, however, recognize the value of conscientious objection
to military service as a witness against the state's absolute claim to righteousness.
His attitude to pacifism has always been complex.

[3] On what follows cf. C. C. West, *Communism and the Theologians*, ch. 4

of universal self-interest and was prepared to use force to overthrow the bourgeoisie rather than attempt to "convert" them (an impossible hope) altruistically to renounce their power and privilege in favour of the workers.

Yet as time went by he realized the degree to which Marxism too must come under the judgement of God. For whilst it affirmed the depravity of men it claimed that one class—the proletariat— was basically good, and hence that it (or its "representative", the Party) was worthy to take power and could infallibly exercise justice. Whilst it recognized the irrelevance of excessive idealism about the degree of justice possible in this world it claimed that one age—the Utopia of true Communism—would achieve perfect justice, and that the toleration of injustice now was a small price to pay for this Golden Age. And in Stalinist Russia Niebuhr saw new horrors committed in the name of this absolute pretension of righteousness and absolute hope for the future, horrors as great as any committed in the name of feudal order or bourgeois liberty.

The result of this discovery was a certain gradual move to the Right in Niebuhr's political thinking and allegiance. From playing a major part in the small American Socialist Party before the Second World War, he became a leading light in the group of "realistic" liberals known as Americans for Democratic Action. And whilst never afraid to deflate the pretensions of his own nation he came to lay more and more emphasis on the values of American liberal democracy.

This comes over, for example, in the later pages of Volume II of *The Nature and Destiny of Man*.[1] In discussing the possibilities of a just social order in history he commends a society in which there is a "balance of power" such that the absolute pretensions of any one group or class are held in check: the very ideal of the Founding Fathers of the U.S.A. In the clash of competing interests, in the marketplace where all absolute claims and pretensions are shown to be relative and finite, a rough truth and justice will be found.

Now this thesis reads, on the political and cultural level, just a little like the doctrine of *laissez-faire* on the economic level. Niebuhr, to be sure, has never been a supporter of pure economic *laissez-faire*; indeed, his part in bringing the Churches to accept

[1] ch. 9, especially, pp. 265ff.

and support Roosevelt's New Deal policies can hardly be over-
estimated. He reminds us not infrequently that the ideals of
"liberty" and "equality" are in permanent tension within history
and that the liberal ideal needs to be constantly challenged by the
socialist critique of a system which gives rise to such inequalities.[1]
Yet for all this refusal to be tied down to pure liberalism one senses
throughout his deep loyalty to the ideals of 1776—in their pessi-
mistic form (the balance of power as a restraint on sins) to be sure,
rather than in the optimistic form which linked freedom so closely
with virtue; but nevertheless reflecting a perhaps uncritical
confidence in the goodness of the ideals themselves. And one
takes the point of Charles West's criticism[2] that this whole ethical
construction of Niebuhr's may turn out to be a purely American
ideology, unable to cope with revolutionary challenges in other
parts of the world.

This "Americanism" is developed rather interestingly in his
later work, *The Irony of American History*. In this book (as in his
"vindication of democracy", *The Children of Light and the Children
of Darkness*) he takes up the theme that pragmatism makes better
sense than moral idealism; for the practice of American democracy
is better than its theory. American ideals ("the land of the free",
"the last best hope of earth") are pretentious, and the officially-held
laissez-faire economic policy which goes with those ideals invites
the just condemnation of the Communists; but in practice America
has shown a commendable flexibility, not only in her internal
economic life (now far from consistently *laissez-faire*) but also
in her foreign policy. For this reason, because she can act prag-
matically and flexibly—not because she is especially righteous or
blessed by God—she is fitted to keep at bay the menace of
international Communism; a menace (he would say) not because
its different ideals are any less worthy than those of America,
but because its utopian absolutism has led to inflexible policies at
home and overseas and to the sanctioning of oppression and terror
in the name of those ideals.

In his last major book, *The Structure of Nations and Empires*,
Niebuhr went a long way towards justifying imperialism in
general—and American imperialism in particular—as a necessary
evil for the sake of world order; *this*, he would say, is what "balance

---

[1] e.g. *Nature and Destiny of Man*, Vol. II, pp. 254f.
[2] West, op. cit., pp. 168ff.

of power" means on the international scene today. Yet he remained
critical of American pretensions, and by 1967 (when I was privi-
leged to hear him speak on the subject of the Vietnam war) he
was perceptibly shifting to the Left again, viewing that war as a
sign that America had already overreached herself, and that this
society was perhaps not, after all, capable of playing the role which
history seemed to have assigned to her.

Whether or not his social ideals thus changed, we must
conclude that, at the height of his career and in the most important
period of his thought, Niebuhr saw the ideal society as one based
on a balance of power (within itself, and over against other nations),
sitting a little loose to ideals, following pragmatic rather than
absolutistic policies. Such a society—which he saw at least in
germ in America—was necessary, to be sure, because of man's
sin, to keep in check the temptation to pride; we shall see the same
vision recurring, paradoxically but not without reason, in the work
of later theologians who would express their view of man rather
differently.

It will be clear from all that I have said that Niebuhr does have
a kind of doctrine of progress. The emphasis on man's sin and
God's judgement might lead one to expect that, whatever progress
he might admit on the purely material level, he would deny that
man's capacity for love and justice, his conquest of moral evil,
in any way grows within history. Indeed, he insists that the Kingdom of God is beyond history; that is what the symbols of the
Second Coming and the Last Judgement are meant to say to us.
And for some of Niebuhr's critics—notably Daniel Day Williams[1]
—this "perfectionism", this insistence on viewing all good in
terms of the *perfect* Good which can only lie in eternity, makes it
impossible for him adequately to evaluate the real progress, from
less to *more* perfect good, which does occur within history.

A Niebuhrian theology could indeed lead to this conclusion,
and it undoubtedly has done so in some of his followers. The
British historian Herbert Butterfield, for example, in his book
Christianity and History, takes a line very closely parallel to—
and probably influenced by—Niebuhr in asserting that all that
history reveals about human life is its inherent sinfulness and God's
judgement upon it. To be sure, Butterfield discerns a providence

---

[1] "Niebuhr and Liberalism" in Kegley and Bretall (eds.), *Reinhold Niebuhr*;
cf. Williams, *God, Grace and Man's Hope*, ch. 3

in history, but it is the work of God, not of man;[1] and he comes to the highly conservative conclusion—reminiscent of Adam Smith's doctrine of the Invisible Hand—that the vocation of the Christian, in social and political issues, is to "stick to his last"; quietly to cultivate loving personal relationships and to avoid pretentious involvements in social action. Thus, he says, the Christian will be co-operating with Providence better than those who arrogantly try to play God and force Providence on its way.[2]

It would be grossly unfair, however, to suggest that Niebuhr himself takes quite such a negative position. His essays on the implications of Barth's theology (collected in Part III of *Essays in Applied Christianity*) show how critical he is of such "transcendental irresponsibility". It is true that at this stage (these essays were written in the early 1930s) he is profoundly sympathetic to the idea that the doctrine of progress may be "little more than dogma", that history is merely "the sorry tale of new imperialisms supplanting old ones".[3] It is true that the only rationale he here gives for Christian social action is that "each generation has the task of defeating its own lusts".[4] But at least he assumes that this struggle is not only to some degree possible but also worthwhile. Even if he is suggesting that history is merely *the history of moral effort*, in which the human will is isolated as the sole object of attention (we shall have to return to this question), at least *this* history has a certain meaning.

In his important book *Faith and History* he develops further his attitude to progress. To be sure, he is highly critical still of the liberal faith in progress, but he is at least able to affirm that there are "provisional meanings" and "renewals of life" in history, as well as "provisional judgements".[5] None of these can be seen clearly for what they are until the End, the final fulfilment and judgement; but they are there nevertheless, and the Christian, like the Old Testament prophets, must try to evaluate them. Yet always the stress is on the provisional. the relative. "Biblical thought recognizes the tentative and obscure patterns of meaning in history; but it never sees them consistently fulfilled in history itself".[6]

Over-confidence in progress, he believes, is demonic.

[1] Butterfield, *Christianity and History*, ch. 5   [2] Butterfield, op. cit., p. 137
[3] Niebuhr, *Essays in Applied Christianity*, p. 143   [4] ibid., p. 146
[5] Niebuhr, *Faith and History*, p. 243   [6] ibid., p. 126

The uncritical confidence in historical development as a mode of redemption may have . . . contributed to our present disaster by heightening the historical dynamism of Western civilization to the point where it became a demonic fury.[1]

Yet the biblical attitude to history, unlike that of classical and oriental cultures, is that it is real and not illusory, and has a meaning and direction. Unlike modern liberals, however, the biblical writers claim that redemption in history is possible only through God's forgiveness; that "even men and nations, thus redeemed, are never free from the taint of rebellion against God";[2] and that evil grows alongside the good and will be manifested in its most demonic proportions at the Last Day.

Niebuhr does affirm, then, that there is a real growth of good in history, even though it is always mixed with evil. What is this good? What is the true and right direction of progress, in Niebuhr's eyes?

From all that we have observed in his other writings, we must assume that it is a progress towards the kind of society in which human pretensions are held most firmly in check; in which idealisms and absolutisms are most easily unmasked for the ideologies which they so largely are; and in which pragmatism is more highly regarded than the imposition of transcendent principles. That is to say, on Niebuhr's assumptions, the perfect liberal democracy. For such a society, he would seem to believe, manifests most clearly, through its limitation of power and its commonsense approach to life, the hard facts of man's finitude and sinfulness and the need for judgement and grace. And this—the bringing of men to an existential awareness of finitude, sin, judgement, and grace— is all that matters; it is the purpose of human life.

Only thus can I understand what Niebuhr says about progress in Chapter seven of the second volume of *The Nature and Destiny of Man*. As we have seen, he affirms in that book the indeterminate possibilities of the development of brotherhood in history; but he certainly does not build this up into a consistent doctrine of progress. In this later passage, after claiming vehemently that "we have learned . . . that history is not its own redeemer", and seemingly rejecting all faith in progress, he goes on to say, "historical circumstances may be more or less favourable to the inducement of

[1] Niebuhr, *Faith and History*, p. 15   [2] ibid., p. 31

that 'godly sorrow' which worketh repentance."[1] *This*, it would seem, is his idea of meaning in history; it is, or can be, a *praeparatio evangelica*, pointing man to the gospel (understood in the narrow sense of sin, judgement, and forgiveness). Thus far, in the passage under discussion, he will go with the Renaissance in assigning a meaning to history, but the meaning itself must be seen through the eyes of the Reformation. History is the story of the Prodigal Son; it (and nature even more) is merely the stage on which the drama of sin and forgiveness is played out.

Is not a whole dimension of Christian hope missing here, we may ask? "The *whole creation*", wrote Paul, that great preacher of sin and forgiveness, "groans and travails" for redemption.[2] But for Niebuhr, as for Kant, it would seem that the only good thing is a good will, and all the rest of the cosmos is merely the background to the working out of the fate of the human will in its grandeur and misery. Like so many theologians today, he divides rigorously the realms of "nature" and the "impersonal" on the one hand and "history" and the "personal" on the other;[3] and if his discussion of this issue, and in particular of the relationship between "naturalistic" Greek and "historical" Hebrew world views in the Christian tradition, is more sophisticated than that of Cox and others,[4] still the dualism remains. And this interpretation of history in an "inward" sense—the history of the human will—creates an even greater gulf between "outer" and "inner" worlds. If, in the last analysis, God's purpose for creation is merely the forgiveness of sins, the transformation of the will and the spirit of man; if he is not concerned about redeeming the "impersonal" structures of society, and even nature itself; then it is hard to see what kind of progress can be affirmed in history.

This, then, is a basic weakness in Niebuhr's thinking. Though he is more sophisticated in his understanding of the corporate structures of society than were some of his Social Gospel predecessors, and though his concern for Christian social action is much greater than that of his continental neo-orthodox counterparts, he is at heart a kind of existentialist. The predicament of man in the face of his finitude—man conceived almost as a disembodied will—man faced with the choice between self-assertion and the acceptance

[1] *Nature and Destiny of Man*, Vol. II, p. 206
[2] Romans 8.22   [3] e.g. *Faith and History*, ch. 2
[4] *Nature and Destiny of Man*, Vol. II, chs. 1–2

of grace; this is his subject matter, and all other dimensions of reality are merely a backcloth. We shall see later what new possibilities emerge when the whole of reality—nature, history, and the inner life of man—is considered as a total process. For the moment we shall merely raise the question whether Niebuhr's world view is an adequate basis for a contemporary expression of the Christian hope, and whether that ideological conditioning for which Charles West criticizes him may not be traced back to the lack of a positive metaphysic and the inadequacy of a pragmatic and quasi-existentialist approach to social issues.

None of these criticisms must be taken to suggest that Niebuhr's contribution to the debate about progress has been minimal or negative. In interpreting to us afresh the great categories of sin, judgement, and grace as clues to history; in proclaiming the Christian faith as "a citadel of hope built on the edge of despair";[1] he has spoken, as powerfully as Barth but more directly and relevantly, to the condition of a difficult and painful period in Western history. For many, agnostic as well as Christian, he has lit up the dark places of history in a new way. Otherwise how can one explain his widespread influence?

For there have been few examples of Christian social thought over the past thirty years which have not revealed a debt to Niebuhr. In British theology one can cite the work of Butterfield already mentioned. One must take note, too, of the works of Mr. Denys Munby, the economist, which are directly relevant to the later themes of this book.[2] Here is a Christian who, naturally concerned that his fellow-believers should be able to affirm and evaluate economic progress, yet makes the category of sin central in his theological analysis, and ends one of his books with the ringing eschatological affirmation of St Bernard:

Hora novissima, tempora pessima sunt, vigilemus.[3]

In the writings of such Church historians as John Oliver[4] and

---

[1] *Moral Man and Immoral Society*, p. 62

[2] Especially *God and the Rich Society* and *Christianity and Economic Problems*

[3]   The world is very evil,
        The times are waxing late,
        Be sober and keep vigil, . . .

                                (Tr. Hymns *Ancient and Modern*, No. 276)
Munby, *Christianity and Economic Problems*, p. 274

[4] Oliver, *The Church and Social Order*, pp. 187f. and *passim*

Roger Lloyd[1] we find an emphasis (and an evident approval) on the impact of neo-orthodoxy—especially in its Niebuhrian form—on English social theology since the mid-1930s, and its chastening influence both on the naïveté of the surviving liberals and the "unreality and dogmatism" of those Anglo-Catholics who advocated a "return to Christendom" and identified the Christian social order with an eccentric up-dating of medieval politics and economics.[2]

Yet Niebuhr's influence spreads farther than this. The examples I have given (and one could think of many more) all date from a period of widespread cultural pessimism;[3] are they relevant to a different climate? There are many theologians who affirm that we are now in a period of optimism, and indeed that optimism about society is (by a strange coincidence) central to the Christian Gospel. They make much of Bonhoeffer's cryptic assertion that "man has come of age", and claim that subservience to the providence and judgement of God is a sign of immaturity. Yet these men are more dependent on Niebuhr's categories than might at first appear. To them—the secular theologians—we now turn.

---

[1] Lloyd, *The Church of England, 1900–1965*, ch. 12
[2] For a detailed discussion of the Christendom Group see Oliver, op. cit., ch. 6
[3] Munby's work dates from the mid-1950s when Niebuhr's influence was still strong. Most of Lloyd's work was done at a much earlier period, and Oliver's attitudes must have been formed under the influence of the Niebuhrian tradition. The thinkers whom they discuss, of course, mostly date from the inter-war period

3

The New Optimism:
The Roots of Secular Theology

> By the loss of the unity which is possessed through the form
> of Jesus Christ, the Western world is brought to the brink of
> the void. The forces unleashed exhaust their fury in mutual
> destruction. Everything established is threatened with destruc-
> tion. This is not a crisis among other crises. It is a decisive
> struggle of the last days.

This is not, as might be thought, a quotation from Butterfield
or some other ultra-Niebuhrian. It is the voice of none other than
the so-called founding father of secular theology, Dietrich Bonhoeffer.[1] I cite it here to show that the roots of secular theology
were laid against a background of cultural pessimism and to
introduce my argument that the secular theologians are by no
means so far from Niebuhr as some might think.

On the other hand it must be admitted that secular theology,
as it has evolved, is associated with a new and precarious kind of
cultural optimism. Over-simplified, its thesis is that man has
"come of age" and, with the extension of human reason and
rational control to those areas where superstition yesterday
lurked, he has become free from the tyranny of nature and of the
past. The rapid development of technology has shown that anything is now possible to man; he can indeed create the good society
on earth.

In January 1966 the American journal *Theology Today* published
an essay by the young theologian William Hamilton entitled
"The New Optimism—from Prufrock to Ringo".[2] His theme is

[1] Bonhoeffer, *Ethics*, p. 105
[2] Reprinted in Hamilton and Altizer, *Radical Theology and the Death of God*.
I do not propose to discuss here the relationship between "secular theology"
and "death-of-God theology"; to those who know the literature it will, I think,

that the pessimism of T. S. Eliot (creator of the rather morbid character J. Alfred Prufrock) and of Niebuhr and the Barthians is outdated. No longer is Western culture afraid; new technological developments have opened up exciting and unlimited possibilities. The Beatles' film, *A Hard Day's Night*, symbolizes for him the new mood of "celebration and rejoicing". But he finds this mood not only in the popular arts but in politics too; the hopefulness of the civil rights movement is a case in point. And he links this mood with the cultural phenomenon of the "death of God"; tragedy, he says, is no longer possible, for tragedy presupposes a tension between the world-as-it-is and a transcendent Good—in which nobody feels the need to believe any more. Secularization—the pushing of God out of the world, the carrying on of everyday life without reference to the divine—has broken the tension which made tragedy possible; and secularization is here to stay, and it is good. We are free, free from bondage to "religion", free to enjoy the world, and to transform it in hope.

It may seem odd to us, looking back after only a few years, that Hamilton should dismiss the Vietnam War as a minor thorn in the flesh and see the race problem as merely a small hurdle to be jumped, adding a little zest and challenge to the onward march of progress. It may seem odd that there should be no reference to the assassination of President Kennedy or to the continued "balance of terror" between the two nuclear super-powers. Yet it is reasonable to believe that in the late 1950s and early 1960s just such an optimism was indeed evolving in America, riding on the wave of the nation's fantastic technological progress. Parallels may perhaps be detected in other countries, in such significant cultural symbols as Harold Macmillan's 1959 election slogan "You've never had it so good". Symbols of tragedy or sheer hopelessness might still appear in the world of the arts,[1] but the artists' traditional exploration of the inner life of man

---

[1] For a Christian comment on some contemporary drama cf. K. M. Baxter, *Speak what we feel*. Whilst theological interpretation of the arts (a field in which I claim no competence) seems to be in perpetual danger of an oversimplified twisting of artists' statements to Christian uses—such as looking for "Christ-figures" everywhere—the importance of this cultural material, so different from that in which the secular theologians seem most interested, can hardly be denied

---

be clear that Hamilton is fairly close to Cox in his main affirmations, whereas Altizer differs at many points from the whole secular tradition

C

would doubtless be included in Harvey Cox's dismissal of existentialism as a morbid bourgeois flight from social responsibility.[1]
It is indeed the world of the Beatles,[2] rather than that of Beckett,
with which the secular theologians feel they have to come to terms.

Harvey Cox's book *The Secular City*, whilst lacking the broad
scope and careful scholarship of, say, Arend van Leeuwen's
Christianity in World History, may be taken as a typical example
of the thinking of the secular theologians. Despite many inconsis-
tencies (some of which we shall have to analyse in detail) a clear
theme runs through the book, a theme which has caught the
imagination of many young Christians and has profoundly influenced theological thinking and Church strategy in the past
few years. It is this. Secularization—defined as "the loosing of the
world from religious and quasi-religious understandings of itself,
the dispelling of all closed world views, the breaking of all super-
natural myths and sacred symbols"[3]—is now widespread in Western
culture and is spreading to all parts of the world. All the absolutes
which once governed life—the location of men in hierarchical
structures in small, static communities, as well as the governing
of public and private life by transcendent principles—are breaking
down and are being replaced by a new, fluid, and open-ended
kind of society. The symbol of this is the vast, technologically-
based metropolitan city, where the style of life may be characterized
by the qualities of "anonymity", "mobility", and "pragmatism",[4]
all of which give man a new kind of freedom—from the past,
from a static form of community-life, from slavish acceptance of
the *status quo* as God-given.

Cox accepts these generalizations as fact. But he attempts also
to show that such a style of life is in accord with the Christian
gospel. How does he do this?

First of all he argues that the Judeo-Christian tradition,[5]
because of its essentially iconoclastic nature, challenges everything

[1] H. Cox, *The Secular City*, pp. 251–3
[2] But cf. the beginning of Chapter IV below   [3] Cox, op. cit., p. 2
[4] Cox, op. cit., chs. 2–3. His fourth characteristic, "profanity", in a sense
includes the other three, in its rejection of interest in "religious" values
[5] It is perhaps significant that this part of his argument (op. cit., ch. 1) is
based almost entirely on *Old* Testament exegesis. Perhaps (as we shall see others
arguing later) the New Testament faith is *post*-secular and even demands a
sort of "re-sacralization". For a critique of Cox's exegesis see W. G. Peck,
"The Secular City and the Bible" in D. Callahan (ed.), *The Secular City
Debate*

in human experience, other than God—nature, the political order, the accepted ethical system, even "religion"—which may set itself up as an absolute. Like Niebuhr, he believes that Christianity can have no truck with any idolization of finite ideals or programmes, and he warns often lest secularity should turn into "secular*ism*", a new kind of closed, absolutistic world view.[1]

But furthermore he notes that the secular society puts supreme value on *freedom*; freedom, as we have seen, from the past, from the bonds of static community, from slavery to absolutes. And he suggests that this gift of freedom—the freedom of man over his environment, which to be sure involves a concomitant responsibility—is closely related to that gift of freedom from the bondage of past sins and from the "powers" which dominate man's life, of which St Paul speaks as the essence of the gospel.[2]

From all this it would appear that Cox has a clearly delineated doctrine of progress. Man is moving from a state of less freedom to a state of more freedom; from a state of "ontocracy" (a static, absolutistic way of life) to one of "technocracy" (a pragmatic, technical, matter-of-fact life-style);[3] from a state of lesser to a state of greater control over his environment (including, it would seem, the human factors in that environment).[4] And this movement, it appears, even though it is a movement away from "religion" and towards "secularity", is in fact a product of the dynamic faith of the Bible, breaking in on the static world view of Eastern and classical cultures,[5] making life open-ended and driving it towards an indeterminate future.

This new way of life—the way of the "secular city"—we shall have to analyse more closely later on, to see whether it will bear the theological weight that Cox places upon it. But in any case it

[1] Cox., op. cit., pp. 20f. Some commentators—e.g. J. Macquarrie in *God and Secularity*, p. 20—suspect that the distinction between secularity and secularism is a rather precarious one

[2] cf. Cox, op. cit., pp. 127ff. and *passim*

[3] For these terms cf. A. T. van Leeuwen, *Christianity in World History*

[4] ". . . we should never (today) seriously ask 'Is New York City governable?' or 'Can nuclear war be prevented?' or 'Can racial justice be achieved?' " Cox, op. cit., p. 129

[5] Macquarrie (op. cit., pp. 53f.) and other commentators ask whether Cox has not over-estimated the biblical contribution towards the rise of science and technology and the modern attitude to nature, *vis-à-vis* that of the Greeks. The writings of A. N. Whitehead (e.g. *adventures of Ideas*) show an extremely sensitive interpretation of the marriage of Greek and Hebrew world views and their influence on modern technological culture

is clear that he affirms this secularity as a Christian ideal, as well
as to some degree an actual state of affairs which is dominating
human life at an ever-increasing rate. Is the Christian doctrine
of progress, then, a belief in and hope for the indeterminate
increase of the secularization process? Is the (fully) Secular City
the Kingdom of God?

Here Cox displays a puzzling ambiguity. At one stage in his
argument he speaks of the secular city as at least a "symbol" of
the coming Kingdom, and he deals ably with all the objections of
those who see the Kingdom as something purely "heavenly" and
in the future, and dismiss the secular city as something all too
"earthly".[1] But in certain other passages in *The Secular City*
itself, and most clearly in a later reply to his critics,[2] he denies
that he is propounding such a simple view; secularization is not
as such the Kingdom, it is neither good nor evil, except in so far
as it "raises the stakes" and poses more starkly God's challenge to
man to be mature.[3]

At the same time it is clear that he sets a high value on secularity
as at least an important element in human progress. In the passage
just mentioned, whilst alluding to Niebuhr and acknowledging
his debt to the latter's thought, he insists on a more positive affirmation than Niebuhr could give of the real signs and foretastes of
the Kingdom within history. And as we have seen, he regards
man's increasing freedom and autonomy as being intimately
related to the gospel's own promise of freedom.

Moreover, he is quite explicit in tracing through history a
pattern of progress—progress from a less secular to a more secular
way of life, from static, religious tribalism to dynamic, pragmatic
urbanism. And whilst he at times suggests that the progress from
"tribe" to "town" to "city" may not be absolutely direct and
linear,[4] it is clear that this three-stage pattern of progress is
roughly equivalent to religious—rather secular—very secular. He

---

[1] Cox, op. cit., pp. 110–14

[2] Cox, "Afterword", in D. Callahan (ed.), *The Secular City Debate*

[3] ibid., p. 192. In certain places in *The Secular City* he states clearly that the
secularization process is intended merely to make possible the achievement of
a "goal" other than itself. This goal, however, is in no way God-given or God-
commanded, but must be devised and worked out by man himself. cf. *The
Secular City*, p. 109

[4] cf. his suggestion that tribe and city may be "two forms of communal-
collective existence" with town individualism in between (*The Secular City*,
p. 12). He never really follows through this suggestion

would hardly accept the contention of the Catholic Left[1] and others that the new form of society, the technopolitan world view, might require a "re-sacralization" of culture.

So for all practical purposes I think we can say that Cox regards progress, from a Christian point of view, as identical with, or at least intimately related to, increasing secularization. We shall see later exactly how this links up with the Niebuhrian tradition which Cox has received. But in order to understand more fully Cox's doctrine of progress and his ideas about "religion" and "secularization", we must look briefly at his intellectual antecedents, both sociological and theological.

In the sociological sphere Cox clearly stands in the succession which stems from Auguste Comte and is represented magisterially by Max Weber.[2] Comte, as is well known, saw the history of mankind as a history of the increasing dominance of human reason over nature and superstition; and his continuum of "religious", "metaphysical", and "positive" stages in human thought is surely the origin of Cox's delineation of the tribe–town–city movement as religious–metaphysical–secular.[3] Weber too emphasized a similar understanding of social change from a similarly idealistic standpoint,[4] tracing through history the process of the "disenchantment of nature",[5] and the movement from a "traditional" through a "charismatic" to a "rational" or "bureaucratic" ordering of society. Whilst he did not affirm the goodness of this process of "rationalization" as unequivocally as Cox affirms secularization,[6] he certainly believed that such a process was taking place, that it was irreversible, and that it was of central importance in humanity's march through time.

---

[1] See B. Wicker, *Culture and Theology*, ch. 4, and the next chapter in the present work

[2] On what follows see further my article "City Man" in *Frontier*, Spring 1968; the reply of D. Martin in that issue, and others of his writings, including *The Religious and the Secular*

[3] cf. *The Secular City*, p. 245

[4] Sociologists discussing theories of social change are wont to set Weber against Marx, the one asserting that ideas and beliefs change the structures of society, the other that ideas are largely a product of socio-economic changes. This distinction between the two approaches is an over-simplification, but has its uses in analysis. Despite some signs of the Marxist position in Cox, he is basically an idealist and a Weberian

[5] A phrase originating from Schiller and beloved by Cox. Cf. H. H. Gerth and C. W. Mills (eds.), *From Max Weber*, pp. 51, 155

[6] Gerth and Mills, op. cit., p. 126

Some sociologists would lay less emphasis than the Weberian
school on the degree and significance of change in society.[1]
Others would agree with Weber, not only in his analysis of social
change but in his rather negative evaluation of it which Cox does
not share. Still others, of course, would follow a quasi-Marxist line
in seeing change as an economically determined process; and these
men might question whether the "secular" society (which by
definition excludes all utopianisms including Marxism) was the
proper end term of such a process, or merely a bourgeois ideology.
And then there might be others again who would see all these
varied insights into the nature and direction of change as by themselves inadequate, and would seek to combine the best in all of
them in a wider vision of the destiny of man. Certainly the "sociology" which Cox takes so seriously is but one option among many
positions held by contemporary sociologists.

Let us turn now to the theological tradition behind Cox, for
here if anywhere we may be able to discover his true relationship
to the thought of Niebuhr, how many of the latter's strengths and
weaknesses he shares, and what if any new contribution he has to
make to the debate about progress.

The theological demand for a critique of "religion", both as
an unbiblical ideology and as an outlook untenable by modern
man, goes back of course to Barth and Bonhoeffer.[2] For the whole
Barthian tradition, "religion" is contrasted sharply with "revelation" and the appropriate response of faith; the former is man's
sinful grasping after God, the latter God's gracious coming to
man and man's humble response. Leaving aside the much debated
question as to whether this distinction is adequate to deal with
the theological problem of religion,[3] we may observe a parallel

[1] cf. the discussion between Cox and Father A. Greeley in *The Secular City
Debate*; Greeley is a good representative of the functionalist tradition in sociology, which sees society in terms of a fairly stable set of "structures" fulfilling
inalienable "functions". On the various schools of contemporary sociology,
to which I allude in this paragraph, G. Winter's important book *Elements for
a Social Ethic* should be read.

[2] The basic documents are Barth, *Church Dogmatics* 1: 2, pp. 280-361, and
Bonhoeffer, *Letters and Papers from Prison*, which must, however, be read against
the background of such of his other works as *The Cost of Discipleship* and *Ethics*

[3] The literature on this is now vast. Tillich, *Systematic Theology*, Vol. III,
passim, presents a useful quasi-Barthian phenomenological perspective. On the
current debate see especially J Macquarrie, *Principles of Christian Theology*,
ch. 7, and *God and Secularity*; J. E. L. Newbigin, *Honest Religion for Secular
Man* and *The Finality of Christ*

with Niebuhr's assertion that it is precisely man's highest ideals, his noblest strivings, which are most easily corrupted by pride; so that religion, morality, and reason are all liable to become demonic. It is far from difficult to adduce examples from history of the use of religion as an ideology to justify the self-assertion of individuals and groups. In theory it might seem that the man whose attitude to ultimate reality is one of humble receptivity, who accepts "revelation" and "justification" from above and builds no great doctrinal, liturgical, or ethical Towers of Babel—such a man would be less likely to be prone to pride and hence to vitiate his other achievements by the corruption of his will.

Now Cox clearly believes that the process of secularization may serve this purpose of controlling pride. This may seem a strange assertion to make in the light of his affirmation of technological achievement, his celebration of man as the "master of things", and his conviction that the Church has too long condemned pride and that the cardinal sin is really its opposite, sloth.[1] Yet his argument seems to be that human technical achievement, and a legitimate pride in it, are not to be feared—unless they are pressed into the service of a religious or other absolute. The secular temper of the age, he would argue, is "realistic" enough to deflate false pride.

Of course Barth was not so naïve as to imagine that his principles about "the abolition of religion" could be applied *tout court* to the life of the Church. Christianity, he says, is inevitably a religion; to pretend that it is, or could be, purely God-given, free of human constructions, would be a false idealism.[2] Indeed, it is the "true religion"; but only through God's judgement and grace, not through any inherent qualities of its own. Barth's principle, then, does not involve an idealistic disavowal of all religion in the name of the purity of the Christian faith; rather it seeks to keep religion constantly under judgement—a thing much to be desired.

It is evident that Cox's more thoroughgoing rejection of "religion" could lead, even on Barthian principles, to a new and

---

[1] Cox, *God's Revolution and Man's Responsibility*, ch. 2

[2] Barth, *Church Dogmatics*, loc. cit. In some of his shorter polemical writings he seems to take a more idealistically anti-religious (and especially anti-Catholic) stance. It is arguable that some of these writings—such as his notorious essay on "The Church" in the first of the preparatory volumes for the Amsterdam Assembly of the World Council of Churches—have been more influential than his more systematic work

terrible ideology. The "religionless Christian", sincerely believing that his "faith" and world view come from God alone unsullied by the ambiguous achievements of human religion, has few resources with which to check his pride. He may indeed have a deep sense of being under judgement for failing to achieve his ideals in the spheres of thought, Church life, and social action; but the ideals themselves—or perhaps I should say the one ideal of secularity —are beyond criticism. Might it not almost be better if an overtly absolutistic ideology were retained, rather than this covert form?[1]

We must now examine more closely Bonhoeffer's view of religion, on which the secularizers base their ideas about "religion-less Christianity", and which has more direct relevance to our problem of progress. For "religion", as Bonhoeffer defines it, is precisely that which hinders "man's coming of age"; which prevents him from taking full responsibility for his environment; which hence is an obstacle to progress, and from which twentieth-century man is shaking himself free. And this "religion" he depicts as having three major characteristics—a metaphysical view of reality, an obsessive concern with the "inner life" and belief in a *deus ex machina*.[2]

First, religion has a metaphysical view of reality. It looks at the world in terms of a set of *a priori* categories which have little to do with the categories of everyday experience. The "real world" for the religious man thus tends to be this transcendent metaphysical construct; what goes on in the everyday world is of little importance. Such an attitude is clearly not calculated to give any impetus to social, technological, or any other kind of change.

Second, religion is concerned with the "inner life" and with individual salvation. The sphere of politics and economics are of no interest to it; it is "what a man does with his solitariness" (Whitehead).[3] Consequently its approach to sin is one which

[1] The parallel with the problem of "value-freedom" (Weber's *Wertfreiheit*) or scientific objectivity in sociology is interesting; for here too "secularity", whilst having its uses, is now seen by many as neither totally possible nor entirely desirable. As Winter (op. cit.) shows, an implicit world view, with its attendant hierarchy of values, lies behind the work of each sociological school

[2] These three characteristics are singled out from the central pages of *Letters and Papers from Prison*, both by G. Ebeling in his essay on Bonhoeffer in *Word and Faith* and by R. H. Fuller in "The World Come of Age: a second look at Bonhoeffer" in W. Nicholls (ed.), *Conflicting Images of Man*

[3] It should be said that this famous quotation was not entirely characteristic of its author, and is certainly not so of many of his disciples. See below, ch. 5

emphasizes the "secret sins" of the individual, not least his sexual aberrations; and the result is not only a tendency to a sort of vicarious voyeurism on the part of clergy (and psychiatrists, whom Bonhoeffer denounces bitterly), but leads to an over-emphasis on what he calls the "sins of weakness" as against the "sins of strength". Discussing Napoleon's part in the drama of human sin, he does not think it of major consequence that this militaristic tyrant was also an unfaithful husband! Bonhoeffer did *not* believe that man is, or ever could be, free from sin in his responsibility for society and for his environment; rather this "outer world" is precisely where the Church has signally failed in pronouncing the word of judgement—as well as of grace. The parallel with Niebuhr is obvious.

Finally, religion puts its faith in a *deus ex machina*; a "stop-gap God" who intervenes to explain all the mysteries and solve all the problems which man cannot or will not solve himself. Such a God diminishes men's responsibility; they need not investigate problems, or act to solve them, if they believe that God will see to it all. Clearly the man who believes that God, in his own good time, will solve all the world's problems has no incentive to participate in progress.

Bonhoeffer believes that modern man is shaking off the shackles of this immature "religion". He is no longer obsessed with his personal salvation; earth is too interesting for him to bother overmuch about heaven. He looks to science, not metaphysics, to unveil to him the nature of things; and this science, in the famous words of Napoleon's astronomer friend Laplace, "has no need of that hypothesis [God]". God is needed less and less to fill the gaps in scientific knowledge. And towards the problems of the world modern man takes a pragmatic stance; he must solve them himself with the resources to hand, not call in a miracle-working deity.

Now, in all this attack on religion it is clear that Bonhoeffer is rebelling primarily against his German pietist background, which gave his fellow-countrymen no resources with which to understand or deal with the phenomenon of Nazism. Whilst occasionally manifesting his unease at certain devotional practices and aspects of Church organization he by no means denies the importance of the corporate sacramental life of the Church or of personal prayer. Indeed Fuller notes (with a certain Anglican satisfaction) his turning with a new appreciation to some practices of the Catholic tradition which demonstrate the corporate and objective aspects of the Christian faith.[1] And Paul Lehmann[2] emphasizes the importance of the "secret discipline" of sacramental worship and prayer in Bonhoeffer's thought.

For all this Bonhoeffer is essentially a Barthian and hence perhaps excessively critical of the all too "human" elements in Christian life. In some of his earlier works (notably *Life Together* and *The Cost of Discipleship*) he strikes a distinctly anti-humanist pose, in which the life of the Church and of the Christian is shown as "wholly other" than the life of the world—to the extent that Christian ideals of "community" and "love" are said to be totally different from those of other men.[3] His tendency to a moral rigorism, a judgemental attitude towards "the world", is clear throughout his writings and is not really mitigated by his affirmation of secular achievement in the *Letters and Papers*. For when all is said and done "secular man", alone in the universe (or at least living "as if there were no God"), with almost unbearable responsibility, is a singularly austere figure.

Has Bonhoeffer gone too far in his rejection of metaphysics, the *deus ex machina*, and the cultivation of the inner life? In the forms which he sets up as targets for attack these are indeed immature and un-Christian barriers to progress. Yet the need for an overall view of reality, related to empirical knowledge and evolved *a posteriori* rather than *a priori*,[4] is affirmed even by the secular theologian Paul van Buren,[5] and indeed by that militant anti-religious polemicist Bernard Shaw.[6] There is a need too, I would suggest, for a concern with man's inner life—not at the expense of his "outer" life, but in terms of a view of man which breaks down this Cartesian dichotomy between "outer" and "inner"[7]

[1] Fuller, op. cit., pp. 135, 139, 146

[2] Lehmann "Faith and Worldliness in Bonhoeffer's Thought", in *Union Seminary Quarterly Review*, Autumn 1967

[3] Bonhoeffer, *Life Together*, p. 31. On the current debate about the nature of Christian love, initiated by A. Nygren's *Agape and Eros*, see D. D. Williams, *The Spirit and the Forms of Love*

[4] On this see further below, ch. 5

[5] "Bonhoeffer's Paradox", in *Union Seminary Quarterly Review*, Autumn 1967, p. 51

[6] In his Preface to *The Black Girl in Search of God*

[7] cf. e.g. J. Dewey, *Experience and Nature*; G. Hibbert, *Man, Culture and Christianity*. The fact that Christianity—and especially Christian love—must be a matter of "the whole man", inner as well as outer, is amply attested throughout the New Testament; cf. 1 Cor. 13.3

—lest his life be lost in shallow externals. Finally, without a God who in some sense acts to help man—not as a substitute but as a co-operator—what happens to the Christian doctrine of Grace?

Bonhoeffer's critique of religion is important. It speaks to the condition of many "modern men" within the Church. It says things that needed to be said. But it does not go far enough. For it leaves us with a crude "either-or" dichotomy—either other-worldly, superstitious religion, or a secularity which hovers on the edge of the shallow and trivial—which, as we shall see in the next chapter, does not deal adequately with the deepest questions about human life and progress.

It would be unfair to say that Bonhoeffer, and those who follow him, have *no* criteria—other than the neutral ideal of secularization—with which to judge progress. His *Ethics* is built round a "Christological principle", which Ebeling[1] notes as a characteristic of "religionless Christianity". Jesus Christ is the one true reality in the universe; he is the standard by which human life is judged. "The human", often said today to be the basic normative principle of Christian ethics,[2] means "the Christological".

But what does this mean in practice? If the theologian adopts a "Christo-monism", if he has no interest in lesser realities and rejects all the insights of secular philosophical or scientific anthropology,[3] how is this "Christological principle" of human development to be spelled out in relevant concrete terms? This assertion, common among Barthians, of Christ alone as the "really real" does not do justice to the lesser realities of our everyday life; indeed, it violates that very "autonomy of the secular" which they are pledged to uphold. It makes no contact with the actual facts of man's existence in history; its only resource for understanding society, it would seem, is the New Testament, interpreted (inevitably) through the covert prejudices of the exegete. If no principles can be laid down "translating Christ", as it were, into terms of the realities of nature and history; if in fact we are not allowed to construct a world view, a metaphysic, even one with Christ at its centre, what guidelines does the Christian faith give us in our quest for the meaning and direction of life? We are left

[1] Ebeling, op. cit
[2] cf. P. Lehmann, *Ethics in a Christian Context*; and ch. 6 below
[3] Lehmann, op. cit., p. 104 and *passim*

with the vague ideal of secularization—the relativizing of all ideals and principles.

Such then, according to Bonhoeffer and to the secular theologians who follow him, are and should be the presuppositions of secular society. Let us now return to Cox and investigate more fully, in the light of our understanding of secularity, his ideas of society and of social progress.

The society which Cox describes as secular is characterized, it will be recalled, by the marks of anonymity, mobility, and pragmatism. In such a society the individual is free from a too close bond to his immediate neighbours, free to make his own relationships as suits him best. He is free from too deep roots in a local community, free to move where he will. He is free from the domination of abstract, transcendent principles of conduct, free to make decisions on a pragmatic basis about the way he should live and the solutions of social problems.

Now Cox is aware of the dangers inherent in such a society. He sees the unfortunate possibilities inherent in a consistent pragmatism, which might eventually lead men to take a purely utilitarian view of culture and even of their fellow-men.[1] He is aware that man needs the "Law" of institutional arrangements, of regulated communal life, as well as the "gospel" of freedom.[2] Yet these are mere mild negative qualifications of a positive thesis—the ideal of maximizing freedom in society.

It is true also that, when he comes to applying this ideal, he sees the need for compromise. For example, a pragmatic approach to the problem of urban government may necessitate greater centralization of power (which would seem to be a restriction of freedom).[3] However, within a "framework" which may thus be more rigidly controlled by governmental institutions than a *laissez-faire* theorist would like, the individual is still free to be anonymous and mobile. Furthermore, as by definition a secular society has no overarching objective but allows a plurality of aims,[4]

---

[1] Cox, *The Secular City*, p. 68

[2] ibid., p. 47. This contrast between social institutions as Law, and personal freedom as gospel, is surprisingly reminiscent of the rather negative Lutheran view of institutions as a "dyke against sin"

[3] ibid., pp. 97f., 132ff.

[4] e.g. ibid., pp. 30f. On this see also D. L. Munby, *The Idea of a Secular Society*

these centralized organs of society cannot have any clear overall understanding of their purpose or goal, except in a very limited sense, and would thus seem to be excluded from operating in any areas of life in which ideals are at stake and value-judgements have to be made.

The picture which begins to emerge is that of a society based on a mild form of what some economists call "welfare capitalism". For pragmatic reasons modern society cannot afford to be anarchic, and it must have a framework whereby its resources are directed towards ever greater social justice. (But what is social justice? This is an awkward value-question.) Yet within this framework a premium is still placed on individual freedom. This is not so strongly emphasized as in the heyday of pure *laissez-faire* capitalism, certainly not in the economic sphere; for society concerns itself with the needs of the individual who cannot "get on" financially and provides him with minimal economic security, interfering with the workings of the market to mitigate such hardships.[1] On the social plane, however, the individual is fundamentally isolated, left to make relationships and to "get on" in society as best he can. And whilst this freedom may be indeed experienced as "grace" by those who have an enterprising spirit, a good education, and certain other financial and personal advantages (including, in certain cases, a white skin), it is experienced by many as just the opposite, an unfulfillable *law* of "get on or get out". For the poor or inadequate man in the secular society—especially if he happens to be black—the "American Dream", the possibility of rising from rags to riches, of unlimited opportunities in the financial and every other sector of life, seems like a hoax.[2]

It will by now be clear that, whilst Cox has a clearer vision of the possibilities of progress than did Niebuhr, his vision of society is fundamentally the same as the latter's—and suffers from the same American myopia. An open, pluralistic, or secular society, in which social purpose arises from the struggle of conflicting interests, is indeed free from the evils of absolutism. No human programme—except the programme of secularization itself—is in danger of being confused with the Kingdom of God. Every man

[1] The Welfare State provisions in America, whilst far behind those of Britain, are more advanced than is generally realized

[2] An excellent discussion of the problems this raises, from a sociological point of view, will be found in R. K. Merton's essay, "Social Structure and Anomie", in his *Social Theory and Social Structure*

is (theoretically) given an equal chance to struggle for a purposeful existence for himself and his fellows. No one oppresses him (overtly); he enjoys glorious freedom—freedom from prying neighbours, freedom from the chafing bonds of tradition, freedom from the proponents of absolute principles who claim to speak in the name of God.

But is such a society anything remotely resembling the Kingdom? Can a way of life embodying so much "grace-less-ness" for so many be the ultimate in God's purposes for mankind? Can it be affirmed as so profoundly Christian—or even neutral?

Some Christian thinkers—far from conservative, and far from naïvely utopian—think that it cannot. And they point to trends in society itself, and in a changing culture, which seem to support their contention of the breakdown of the secular ideal. In the next chapter we will examine the thought of these men and the cultural changes which they adduce as evidence for their contentions.

4

The New "Realism":
The Failure of Secular Theology

One Sunday in January 1967—just a year after the publication of
Hamilton's essay on the new optimism—an event of some symbolic significance occurred in a small church on the edge of Harlem
in New York City. A congregational singing-practice was scheduled
to precede the service; and as an introduction to this the organist
played a variation on a strangely familiar melody. It was the
Beatles' new song, "Eleanor Rigby", a lament about alienation
and loneliness; and when he came to begin the practice proper
the organist gave as his reason for playing it the fact that it wit-
nessed to a certain return of a sense of tragedy in Western culture,
and hence to the renewed relevance of the Christian gospel to that
culture.

At this time, indeed, a palpable change of mood was occurring
among many students and others in American society. Those who
opposed the Vietnam war (an increasing number) were beginning
to realize that it was more than a minor peccadillo of a great
nation. As it dragged on and its cost mounted, some were asking:
could it be a manifestation of a fundamental sickness in society?
At the same time Americans were becoming more and more aware
of the magnitude and intractability of the race problem. American
racism looked less and less like what Cox might call "a throwback
to a lost tribalism", soon to be outgrown; it seemed more deeply
ingrained than that. Could it be that this stark, growing, and total
confrontation between the white "haves" and the coloured "have-
nots"[1] was about to prove the crucial point at which the secular

---

[1] Many radical commentators see Vietnam as typical of the wars of oppression
that whites are going to fight against non-white nationalists in the next few
years. For a convincing argument linking America's Vietnam policy to her
domestic racism, see R. Segal, *The Race War*

society would show its flaws, the issue which it could not tackle and which would break it?

It is too early to document adequately this quite recent change in the cultural ethos of American society. What is, however, manifest is the way in which this twin problem of race and poverty—at national and international levels—is obtruding itself on the consciousness of "secular" Western society. And there are good sociological and economic reasons for believing that a "secular"—that is to say, a completely open and pragmatic—society cannot solve these problems from within its own resources.

The problem centres on the "pragmatic" nature of such a society; the temptation to affirm that the "workable"—which in a largely capitalist system means economically viable—is the good. Now, *laissez-faire* capitalism has given rise, for quite good pragmatic reasons, to welfare capitalism—which undoubtedly makes possible a somewhat juster distribution of income. Socialist groups with their "dogmas" of justice and equality have doubtless contributed something to this development; but it is arguable that the primary cause lies in the process of secularization. The "dogma" of *laissez-faire* capitalism collapsed when the problem of the trade cycle proved the unworkability of the existing system. For pragmatic reasons the need was seen to correct the violent swings of the trade cycle by the maintenance of "effective demand"; and this was to be achieved by higher wages, guaranteed benefits for the unfortunates of society, and major government intervention in the economy.[1]

Thus a pragmatically-run economy will tend to increase social justice—*up to a point*; the point where effective demand is sufficient to keep the economy running smoothly. There may still be those—within the country concerned, and in other countries not integrated with its economy—who are left out of this redistributive process. To bring them in, to share some of the resources which the affluent majority of voters in the country concerned is enjoying, is not "practical politics". The eighty per cent (say) who are well off can always outvote the "submerged fifth"—let alone the millions in other countries who have no voice in the counsels

---

[1] The best popular exposition of post-Keynesian economics and their social implications is to be found in the works of J. K. Galbraith; cf. his *The Affluent Society* and *The New Industrial State*. On the worldwide trend towards "pragmatism" in economics see G. Sampedro, *Decisive Forces in World Economics*

of the rich nations. These new poor are *not* needed in the economy.[1] Pragmatism will not bring them in. Only if society is challenged in the name of some absolute moral principle is there any hope that it will shoulder its responsibility.

The question of race, whilst closely related to that of poverty (most poor people in the U.S.A. and in the world are coloured), is perhaps more complex. A "pragmatic" approach would after all seem to demand the giving of equal opportunity to all, whatever the colour of their skin; to reject the skills and gifts of non-whites would seem an inefficient policy, smacking of "unsecular" prejudice. Unfortunately it is not as simple as that; the fact that, after America, the Union of South Africa is one of the world's most prosperous countries shows that racial integration and economic growth need not go hand in hand. Why is this?

It will be recalled that even some social Gospel thinkers believed that evolution had proved the white race to be the fittest to lead the world.[2] Now unfortunately there is a measure of truth in this—*if*, and only if, evolution is understood in the crude nineteenth-century sense of the "survival of the fittest" (in physical —not mental, moral, cultural, or spiritual—terms). For whatever reason—be it climate, religion, or culture—the white races *have* proved the "fittest" in certain areas of life, notably in the sphere of economic progress (and if some of this progress was achieved by the use of black slaves, what did this matter to those for whom aggression was the law of the universe?). The coloured peoples started off with some disadvantage in the economic rat-race; this is not necessarily a shameful thing, indeed it may have helped

---

[1] This is most patently true on the world scale. It is sometimes said that the rich countries should aid the poor ones in order to expand their own markets, i.e. create necessary "effective demand". But for the moment most world trade is between the rich countries; they provide adequate markets for each other's products. Already, too, the rich countries are inventing man-made substitutes for the raw materials they import from the Third World; one can conceive of a situation in which they might not have any economic need for the Third World at all

[2] cf. above, ch. 1. The recent discussions among educationalists about the relative intelligence levels of whites and non-whites, make it *absolutely imperative* that we build a set of values about race which is in no way affected by a possible discovery that non-whites are (in terms of the intelligence required in our kind of society) "less intelligent". The "pragmatic" approach is based on the assumption that different races are equal in *virtually all respects*, and *hence* it is "in everybody's interest" to give them equal chances in every sphere. The basic assumption here may now be proving rather precarious

D

them to preserve their full humanity better than the whites. But this disadvantage places a barrier to their sharing in the world's affluence; and it has been compounded many times by those who, through prejudice, denied them access to a decent education and to that "ladder" of self-advancement around which capitalist society and its values are built. Some racial prejudice is indeed irrational and unsecular, and this could doubtless be abolished by Cox's programme (if only men were as consistently rational as Cox seems to think possible!). But in so far as non-whites are (no shame to them) perhaps less inclined to that acquisitiveness which provides the motive force for a capitalist economy, and in so far as many of them are in fact (through no fault of their own) less well qualified than their white brothers, "pragmatism" is not powerful enough to give them a just place in the affluent society.

It would seem then that a secular society, whilst bringing greater prosperity and a juster distribution of wealth to many, denies these things to many others. This objection to the new social order is quite in addition to another one, perhaps more commonly heard: that "culture", the intangible, immeasurable *quality* of life, is stunted, reduced to "one dimension", in a technological, highly rational society.[1] However far this may be true, it clearly adds to the challenge which the secular society presents to Christians in their struggle for justice and for "wholeness" in human life. How should they respond?

In the rest of this chapter I propose to examine one group of thinkers who, primarily concerned to refute the "secular" ideology, have begun to evolve a theological stance with which to replace it—the English "Catholic Left". In the following chapter I deal with a theological movement which, less concerned to oppose secularization (and indeed sometimes accused of being in league with it), provides fuller and more consistent material for a theological critique of secular presuppositions—the movement loosely known as process-theology.

The Catholic tradition within Christendom, with its emphasis on the corporate and institutional aspects of the Faith, might be expected to be antipathetic to individualism—in its economic, cultural, and other forms. Up until quite recently the Roman

[1] cf. H. Marcuse, *One-Dimensional Man*; B. E. Meland, *The Realities of Faith*, ch. 1 and *passim*

Church (and such Anglo-Catholics as T. S. Eliot[1] and the "Christendom Group") based its social teaching on the medieval idea of a "Christian society" with an economic basis not far removed from feudalism (but emphasizing also the guild-based structure of the urban, mercantile world of the Middle Ages). Gradually it has come round to a greater awareness of the fact of religious and ideological pluralism ("secularity") in all societies; but it has maintained constant, in teaching if not in practice, its anti-capitalistic bias. Gradually its feudal economic principles have evolved into a rather idiosyncratic and highly anti-Marxist kind of socialism and more recently (in such encyclicals as *Pacem in Terris* and *Populorum Progressio*) to a clearer and more highly committed, though still carefully qualified, left-wing stance alongside secular socialistic forces.

Those Roman (and Anglican) Catholics involved in social and political thought and action at the grass-roots have likewise hovered uncertainly between feudalism, socialism, and idiosyncratic communitarian doctrines of their own. We have already noted the half-conservative, half-radical position of the Anglo-Catholic Christendom Group; though it must be said that an important section of the Anglo-Catholic movement around the turn of the century was more clearly socialistic in its political aims, and this movement laid the foundations for the work of William Temple which had such a profound influence on British political life. Adrian Cunningham[2] notes a similar ambivalence, a combination of semi-socialistic ideals with feudal romanticism, in the Roman Catholic social movements in Britian and France in the first few decades of the present century.

But the corporate, communitarian emphasis of Catholic Christianity, whilst it has been used to bolster up feudalism and fascism, can also provide material—along with certain aspects of modern science and philosophy—for a new kind of socialism which poses a thoroughgoing challenge to the secular society whilst refusing to return to the past. The development of such a socialism is the concern of the Catholic Left in Britain.

The Catholic Left—an informal group of laymen and some priests, mostly Dominicans—is deeply concerned about those very

[1] cf. Eliot, *The Idea of a Christian Society*
[2] A. Cunningham, "Culture and Catholicism; a historical analysis", in B. Wicker and T. Eagleton (eds.), *From Culture to Revolution*

problems of race and poverty which the "secular" approach has proved unable to solve. But they go beyond political and economic issues to demand a fundamental restructuring, not just of society itself but of our *view* of society and indeed of our total world view.

Whilst the works of the more activistic members of the group such as Neil Middleton[1] present most clearly this union between new thought and new action, the chief ideologue of the group appears to be Brian Wicker, and to his thought we must pay some attention.

His challenge to the secular society is thrown down dramatically at the beginning of his major work to date, *Culture and Theology*. The secular world view, he says, is based on a Lockean theory of perception which breaks up experience into discrete sense-data and radically separates subject from object, observer from observed; a nominalistic theory of language which likewise drives a wedge between "reality" and the concepts which we use to speak about it and handle it; and a bourgeois theory of society which looks upon men as discrete individuals and "society" or "community" as an abstraction. I will not dwell on his discussion of language, which is rather difficult and not directly germane to our subject; but I must say something on the matter of epistemology before passing on to his social thought.

The secular world view, as we have seen, is highly pragmatic or "commonsensical". It tends to see reality in a prosaic way, in terms of the sense-data impinging on the observer, and the effect of the observer's action in operating upon this "outside world". As with Kant, there is a perpetual problem of the relationship between this "outside world" and the "inner world" of the observer; but in any case the world is viewed in mechanistic terms— a mechanical interrelationship of separate objects, indeed of separate sense-data—and hence reality-as-a-whole is seen in terms of Mind-plus-Machine, with a constant temptation to reduce to Machine anything outside the *individual* mind of the observer or agent. The dehumanizing potentialities of this dualism—man seen as either the almost disembodied, isolated subject of existentialism, or alternatively as an example of a sophisticated kind of machine[2]—are evident.

This world view was largely based on the fundamental assumptions of Newtonian physics, for which the model of the world

[1] N. Middleton, *The Language of Christian Revolution*
[2] cf. F. W. Matson, *The Broken Image*

as a lot of separate lumps of matter interrelating in a mechanistic way proved very useful. New developments in science, however, have rendered such a model largely obsolete.[1] In the new world of Heisenbergian and Einsteinian physics—and in the "field-theories" of modern biology and psychology—the view of reality as fragmented into objectively and mathematically measurable "lumps" appears as a useless and misleading hypothesis. We must now understand our world in terms of *relationships*; some of the new concepts of physics can indeed only be understood as referring to a nexus of relationships, not to separable "things". Moreover, a measure of humility and scepticism, an awareness that not all reality is mathematically determinable, an awareness of the unique and new and even of a "dimension of depth"— these are all manifest in the contemporary philosophy of science.

Wicker's interest is in those philosophical trends (he discusses Merleau-Ponty's phenomenology but he could equally well have taken Dewey, Whitehead, or a host of other thinkers) which take up this theme of reality as relationship and the need for a reintegration of overall human experience in all its richness, as against the reductionist tendencies of "secular" philosophy.[2] We shall see in the next chapter how the process-theologians have likewise seen in modern science some hints towards the possibility of an open, dynamic, and evolving view of reality; here we will simply note the way in which many contemporary philosophical movements are tending towards an affirmation of "wholeness" as against the analytic, fragmentative world view of the past two or three centuries.

This view of reality, and of man's perception of it, has obvious corollaries in the area of our understanding of society. Whilst Wicker does not believe that the idea of "the individual" and his autonomy is either a mere abstraction[3] or valueless (it had its value in helping to break down the static communal order of feudalism)[4] he builds on Marx and on some contemporary

---

[1] cf. I. G. Barbour, *Issues in Science and Religion*, especially ch. 10; B. E. Meland, *The Realities of Faith*, ch. 4. Some of these new ideas are popularly summarized by J. A. T. Robinson, *Exploration into God*, ch. 5. See further below, ch. 5

[2] Further on phenomenology and the Catholic Left see G. Hibbert, O.P., *Man, Culture and Christianity*

[3] cf. Wicker, *First the Political Kingdom*, pp. 52ff.

[4] Wicker, *Culture and Theology*, p. 42

sociologists[1] to show that it is the individual-in-*community* or the "social self" which is the basic reality, the basic unit almost, of human social life. Having shown that the secular theory of society is inevitably individualistic—based on a concern for individual autonomy and integrity—he claims that this is a major weakness in the secularist view of what *is*, and the rest of his work, and that of his colleagues, is dedicated to showing how this basic flaw affects equally the secularist view of what *ought* to be in society.

The Catholic Left is, to be sure, critical of Marx (though more especially of his twentieth-century Communist interpreters).[2] Its representatives feel that Marxism, having got rid of the idea of the abstract individual, too often subordinates *real* individuals to an equally abstract "society" or "State", by means of a political theory which tends to reduce man to a thing, a creature of the economic process (thus compounding, rather than combating, that "alienation" which denies the true, more-than-economic nature of man). For the Catholic Left, therefore, a reformation of "culture"—the way we view the world, our symbolic methods of expressing that view, and a share for all in effective political power and cultural creativity as well as economic capital—is almost more important than an economic reformation of the traditional Communist type, and the latter is certainly of little real human value without the former.

This involves, for Wicker, a rediscovery of "the sacred"; a project which would doubtless horrify Cox. The central category in man's experience of the sacred is seen (following Eliade)[3] as the experience of *participation* in the community of all that is. The Eucharist—effectual symbol of our participation in Christ— is thus seen to be at the heart of Christianity and profoundly relevant to social issues.[4] At the same time this "re-sacralization" does not mean a return to a *pre*-secular mentality; for Wicker notes how the coming of Christ revolutionized the concept of the sacred by "humanizing" it, so that the "sacred place", for example, is now no longer a building but the community of believers,

---

[1] cf. G. Winter, *Elements for a Social Ethic*, ch. 4, on the concept of the "social self" as used by G. H. Mead and others

[2] Wicker, *First the Political Kingdom*, pp. 31f.; C. Taylor, "From Marxism to the Dialogue Society", in Wicker and Eagleton (eds.), *From Culture to Revolution*

[3] M. Eliade, *The Sacred and the Profane*

[4] This is more fully discussed in Wicker, *Culture and Liturgy*

the Body of Christ.[1] And the new form of experience of the sacred, after the collapse of the primitive anti-scientific mentality, now occurs in the context of "the human community itself", rather than any kind of nature-worship or strange inhuman idolatries removed from the world of everyday.[2]

This "humanizing" of the concept of the sacred seems to me to have certain important metaphysical implications, though Wicker fails adequately to spell them out. The major difference between the "pre-secular" and "post-secular" world views would seem to be that the latter's metaphysic is not static but *dynamic*. The "open-endedness" of human existence, the fact that man is never complete but ever becoming and making new, is emphasized by Wicker as an important element in the emerging post-secular philosophy.[3] If this idea of dynamic open-endedness were to be extended to become a general ontological principle, it is clear where the difference would lie between the old and the new metaphysics.

It is, I think, the *static* element in pre-secular religion and metaphysics—the elevation of the "really real" into a timeless eternity above the world of "change and decay" which almost by definition cannot be really important[4]—against which the secularizers legitimately rebel. Such a view of reality certainly gives little impetus to change or progress; what matters is the eternal, the changeless. Yet, if Wicker is right, the secular alternative—the rejection of metaphysics in the name of a total commitment to the immediacy of the empirical here and now—has major weaknesses, in that it fails to do justice to the communal dimensions of man's life and its setting in the whole "society of being". Secularization can indeed motivate change—it almost demands change for change's sake—but it cannot direct it. Hence a new metaphysic is demanded; one based on the categories of change and time as fundamental to our understanding of reality. This type of "process" metaphysic (which the Catholic Leftists do not explicitly espouse, and some of whose exponents they sharply criticize) we shall explore more fully in the next chapter.

What contribution, then, does the Catholic Left have to make to a contemporary theology of progress? How does it fit into the

---

[1] Wicker, *Culture and Theology*, pp. 216f.   [2] ibid., p. 246
[3] cf. Wicker, *First the Political Kingdom*, p. 37
[4] cf. J. Dewey, *Experience and Nature*, especially ch. 2

three-way debate between utopian liberalism, neo-orthodoxy, and secular theology on this issue?

An essay by Wicker on "Eschatology and Politics"[1] is of particular importance here, especially as illustrating the relationship of the Catholic Left to the chastened radicalism of Niebuhr. In this essay he shows how an eschatological stance—a commitment to the Kingdom of God, which is always "beyond" and "ahead" of any existing social order—is essential for Christians in contemporary society. The "secular" accommodation of the Faith to the existing world view is *not* revolutionary; only commitment to a transcendent and future ideal, which radically challenges existing culture and self-understanding, can supply the necessary dynamism for revolutionary Christian "engagement" in the contemporary world. Marxism, like Christianity, has become for the most part "de-eschatologized" and "pragmatic"; it cannot in its traditional form help Christianity to recover its revolutionary stance.[2] A more profound challenge must come from a revolutionary humanism which transcends both the existing social order and any possible or conceivable form of communal life; a humanism pointing towards the "ultimate future", which connects up with the present and the immediate future only *via* the theological and eschatological route of Cross and Resurrection. A social vision which does not come to terms with these stark Christian realities is not worth having.

Now here there is at once a striking similarity to Niebuhr and an important difference from him. The Kingdom of God is not identified with the Kingdoms of this world; it is *always*, not just at the present time, something beyond them, something which challenges to their very depths both overt utopianisms and the covert idolatry of the "secular". Sophisticated political realism is necessary in order to translate the claims of the Kingdom into action in society.[3] The Kingdom in its purity lies the other side of the Cross.

---

[1] In Wicker and Eagleton (eds.), *From Culture to Revolution*

[2] The Catholic Left tends to disparage much contemporary Marxist-Christian dialogue as a conversation between two forms of "secularity", two religions which can only face each other because they are both emasculated. It is sometimes even suggested that an unholy alliance is being formed here between the pragmatic First and Second Worlds against the revolutionary challenge of the Third World. cf. Wicker, loc. cit., p. 279

[3] Wicker, art. cit., p. 293

But this eschatological dimension is not used as an excuse for exalting "the relativistic social order" to pride of place in Christian social thought. Some measure of the realization of the Kingdom in history today is possible—albeit only through death and resurrection, in which the Church as Christ's Body must lead the way.[1] And this Kingdom, as we have seen, is one of *community* rather than one of mere individual freedom and autonomy; so this absolute good, true community, must be affirmed as the goal of Christian social action, over against the loose, relativistic ideal of the secular theologians and Niebuhr.

This attitude of "realistic idealism"—the courage to work towards an absolute good in history even under the judgement of God and amidst the entanglements of sin—is well illustrated by the attitude of the Catholic Left to "situation ethics".[2] Secular theologians, in general, have supported the current movement in ethical theory towards the rejection of absolute "principles" and the advocacy of pragmatic judgement in the concrete ethical "situation".[3] The reasons are obvious. Niebuhr and the secularizers alike refuse to exalt moral principles, formulated by sinful men, into the absolute place of God. Niebuhr (whilst critical of situation ethics as such, and insisting on the need for some moral norms) emphasizes also the impossibility of implementing the absolute law of love in a sinful world, and the need for responsible compromise. The secularizers, with a more optimistic view of human nature, might emphasize more the ability and responsibility of "man come of age" to judge for himself what is right, without running for safety to an absolute moral law which may have demonic effects if applied uncompromisingly. But both Niebuhr and the secularizers would agree in invoking the "Protestant Principle" which rejects the rule of Law in human life as being a false absolute.[4]

[1] ibid., pp. 282–6. What this death and resurrection means in practice for the Church is spelled out as both total and sacrificial commitment to the struggle for justice for those "left out" of the secular society; and also alongside this a measure of "de-institutionalization", not the removal of the "eschatological signs" of ministry, sacraments, and so on but the stripping off of excretions to lay bare their true nature
[2] On what follows cf. Wicker, *First the Political Kingdom*, pp. 91ff.
[3] cf. J. Fletcher, *Situation Ethics*; P. Lehmann, *Ethics in a Christian Context*
[4] The one absolute is said by Fletcher to be "love" (*agape*). For him this *is* directly applicable in ethical decisions. His definition of it, however (roughly, willing the neighbour's good), seems simplistic, devoid of content and rather

Not so the Catholic Left. They are not unaware of the need
for compromise in a sinful world; their belief in the frequent
necessity of conflict, and sometimes violent revolution, to establish
a more just and loving society, should prove that. Yet they would
criticize the "situationists" on two grounds. First, their view
of the "situation" in which moral judgements must be made is
too narrow; like all secular thinkers they fail to fit the individual,
and the immediate situation, into an overall world view—stretching
ultimately through all time and all space.[1] Second, by counselling
accommodation to the "situation", even where this may mean
compromise of traditional Christian ideals, they diminish the
eschatological, revolutionary tension of Christian ethics. It is
the situation that should (where possible) be changed if it is
basically "alienative" and prevents the exercise of love and commitment in the building of true community. The basic principles—
for example, Christian marriage as the ideal sexual relationship—
derived from ultimately metaphysical and theological convictions
about the nature of man, must be upheld; though not, one hopes,
too harshly or pharisaically. This is not to say that these principles
are laid down for all time and do not evolve and change (even
perhaps by precedent, like much positive law); such a world view
as is appropriate for us today cannot, as we have seen, be static
and deterministic. But principles do not dissolve into chaos, or
remove to a level of "impossible possibility", as ethical thinkers
in the Barthian-secular tradition seem to suppose. They must
be maintained as norms, if the Christian ethic is to be truly an
ethic of change and progress and not of *acquiescence*; acquiescence
in the "situation" and ultimately in the whole secular *status quo*.

It would seem, then, that the Catholic Left has a definite
theology of progress. Progress is possible, and it is towards a
definite ideal, one of unalienated community, in which society
and the cosmos can "become what they are". Unashamedly they
hold up this vision as an absolute good; they are prepared to run
the risk of condemnation for idolatry, and the presence of sin

[1] On this see G. F. Woods, "Situation Ethics", in I. T. Ramsey (ed.), *Christian
Ethics and Contemporary Philosophy*. Helen Oppenheimer's brilliant essay on
"Moral Choice and Divine Authority" in the same volume is also relevant to
this topic

---

extrinsic and moralistic. On this topic I would once again refer readers to the
writings of D. D. Williams, especially *The Spirit and the Forms of Love*

in all human ideals, of which they are fully aware, will not compel them to compromise their idealism. This is not an easy utopianism; the Cross hangs over it. But it is a positive vision.

Yet much of the theology and the metaphysic behind this remains, as I have suggested, to be filled in. If the writings of the Catholic Left occasionally strike one—despite their ideal of a community of grace and love rather than of alienative and individualistic moralism—as a little graceless and even pharisaical, it may be because their eyes are so fixed on what *ought* to be and the need for a determined struggle to achieve it that they lack the ability to rest on the grace, the givenness, of what *is*. And here process-theology may have something to contribute, in the basic assumptions about reality and in the ensuing life-style, as well as in some filling-out of the picture of human progress in its actualities and possibilities.

5
Progress and "Process"

The idea that modern scientific discovery might have metaphysical implications is not new. I am not referring to the *anti*-metaphysics of the so-called "scientific world view"—the reduction of reality to what can be measured and analysed, to empirical sense-data—which we have seen to be intimately linked with the "secular" understanding of life. I am thinking rather of those who, before the First World War, saw new discoveries in both physics and biology as pointing to an overall understanding of reality based on the primacy of interrelationships (rather than separable "things") and of open-endedness, newness, and evolution (rather than a deterministic mechanical givenness).

These philosophers—men like Bergson, Lloyd Morgan, Alexander, and above all Whitehead—were ahead of their time. Their often stumbling efforts to establish an empirically-based metaphysic incurred the wrath of all those (idealists and empiricists alike, but especially the latter) who divided reality rigidly between the world of ideas, values, and spirit on the one hand, and the world of science and of sense-data on the other. During the Dark Ages of the inter-war years they were eclipsed by that school of empiricist philosophers who were concerned only with the analysis of language and its testing for meaningfulness against "scientific" verification. Their attempt to marry matter and spirit was equally incomprehensible to those Barthians who sought to shake the Christian faith free from empirical verification and cultural validation.[1]

Today, though still laughed at by empiricist philosophers and suspect to neo-Barthian theologians, this kind of thinking is finding new recognition; not only among theologians and philos-

[1] On all this see I. G. Barbour, *Issues in Science and Religion*, ch. 5. Barbour is essential reading to fill out my deliberately sketchy introduction to Process thought

ophers, but among scientists with no apparent non-scientific axe to grind.[1] Perhaps, as the failure of a purely "secular" approach to life is becoming apparent, this new metaphysic and its religious implications may speak to our condition. Let us examine it a little more closely.

Barbour's book, already cited, sets out very clearly the main themes of "process" thinking.[2] The new atomic physics, centred on such theories as Heisenberg's uncertainty principle and Einstein's theory of relativity, has largely broken down our idea of reality as solid matter, as a machine made up of separate and analysable parts, operating like the proverbial tram "in determinate grooves". The sub-atomic world is constantly found to defy the "laws" of Newtonian physics—and even those of logic ("the same thing cannot be both P and not-P"). Uncertainty, a real element of newness and of mystery, is revealed as operating at the most basic level of reality which science can plumb. Reality at its most basic level is better viewed, say many modern scientists, in terms of "events" and "relationships", rather than discrete "things" existing independently of their location in time-space. And this new emphasis on time has had an effect in biology too. The evolutionary theory, developed since Darwin's time to a considerable level of sophistication, has pointed the way to an understanding of life as evolving rather than given or created once-for-all; and at the same time the barriers between "matter" and "life", and between the different scientific disciplines dealing with them, has seemed increasingly less relevant in the light of developments in organic chemistry and other branches of knowledge.

The impact of this breakdown of specialization upon biology itself has been considerable and is of particular importance for us. For here as in physics the deterministic hypothesis (such as the idea that evolution is really only the unfolding of what was there all the time and not the creation or emergence of the radically new) is now questioned; and also a very considerable qualification of that individualistic hypothesis, on which popular Darwinism based its doctrine of the "survival of the fittest",

[1] cf. E. E. Harris, *The Foundation of Metaphysics in Science*

[2] cf. also B. E. Meland, *The Realities of Faith*, ch. 4. The account there of the impact of Whiteheadian thought on the liberal theologians of Chicago should give food for thought to any who might be tempted, by occasional points of resemblance, to regard process theology as unregenerate liberalism of the Social Gospel type in a new dress

has been found necessary. The way in which modern science is forced to see everything as interrelated, demands that life—animal and human—be seen as a total process, a total *community*, not simply a conglomeration of individuals striving for mastery.[1]

Furthermore this emphasis on interrelationship challenges the vaunted "objectivity" of science. There is a relationship between the observer and the data he observes; he cannot carry out his experiments in lofty isolation, but is himself part of them, and in some fields of research it is vitally important for him to take this fact into account.[2] The scientific approach to life, therefore, cannot be independent of human concerns, commitments, and ideals—what the phenomenologist would call "projects". Objectivity is possible (more so in some disciplines than in others) and has its value; but it is not absolute. We, the observers, as creative participants in reality, create "truth" as much as we discover it.

This possible new scientific understanding of the world thus briefly summarized, may lead to some important philosophical and theological implications. The relative nature of "matter" and the real newness involved in the evolutionary process suggest that there is (to say the least) no need for philosophers to reduce "life" and "mind" to materialistic terms; they can be seen as evolving as new "levels of being". At the same time all these levels are intimately linked; "mind" and "matter" are not ultimately opposed but are two parts of one whole. And the new awareness that "subject" and "object" (in a scientific experiment or any other situation) cannot be split asunder suggests an intimate, two-way relationship between the world of science and the world of human ideas and ideals.

The religious implications of all this, of which the early philosophers (especially Whitehead) were well aware, have been discussed at length in recent years.[3] The process-theologians,

---

[1] This is not to deny a limited validity to Darwin's hypothesis. It merely shows that individualistic self-assertion should not be the central category in understanding the means or the direction of evolution; it may or may not, at various levels, be functional for the well-being of the community as a whole. It is a community—not individual creatures, species, etc.—which is evolving; so the new evolutionary theory claims. The meaning of this complex relationship between the individual and the whole will become clearer as we proceed. cf. Meland, loc. cit.

[2] cf. Barbour, op. cit., ch. 7

[3] For the best detailed discussions see J. B. Cobb, *A Christian Natural Theology*, and B. E. Meland, *The Realities of Faith*. Simpler (and less adequate) analyses

following Whitehead, have suggested that this evolving universe in its complexity points to the need for a Principle of unity in which all things can be held together in dynamic tension, which can evoke and maintain the universal thrust towards creativity and newness. Such a Principle, being the highest Reality of all, must exhibit at least those qualities of personality, self-consciousness, and purposefulness which come to their fruition in man. Hence this Principle, it is suggested, can rightly be called "God".[1]

But can he be identified with the Christian God? One major problem which is raised by process-theology is the implication (based on the ontology of being-in-relationship common to this school) that such a Being, whilst in a sense above and beyond the cosmos, is in a sense affected by it and evolving along with it. Such a denial of the traditional doctrine of God's impassibility and apparent threat to his absoluteness may be construed as dangerous to Christian theism; but other theologians, who would by no means identify themselves with the Process school, have also questioned whether the classical idea of the absolute deity, appropriate within a Hellenistic world view, is either true to the biblical witness or meaningful in contemporary apologetic.[2]

It would, for all this, be too much to claim (as some have been over eager to do) an easy identification between the God of this new "natural theology" and the God and Father of our Lord Jesus Christ. Like all natural theologies, this can only point men to ways of thinking about God. And most Process thinkers emphasize the need for revelation in the form of Christ, the historical "key" to the process, the revealer of its purpose and the opener up of new possibilities in the universal search for communion with God and with others.

[1] cf. Cobb, op. cit., ch. 4, one of the best discussions of Whitehead's arguments for the existence of God

[2] One recent example is J. A. Baker, *The Foolishness of God*, ch. 6. Charles Hartshorne, the much-criticized but always suggestive leading contemporary philosopher of the school, has done much, in *The Divine Relativity* and other works, to establish an approach to the "absoluteness" of God in terms of the totality and depth of his relatedness to his creatures, to which he argues by a sort of *analogia entis* from different levels of relationship within the created order

may be found in W. N. Pittenger, *God in Process* and *Process Thought and Christian Faith*; P. Hamilton, *The Living God and the Modern World*. The best popular exponent of all is certainly D. D. Williams, some of whose work I shall discuss at length later

The philosophical problems inherent in process theology cannot be adequately discussed in a work of this nature. Problems there certainly are, and many of them will arise in the following pages. But it should at least be noted that this approach to understanding the world and the Christian faith may help us to affirm progress in a way that other philosophies and theologies fail to do.

Of course, it does so at a risk. The less we emphasize the "otherness" of God and the more we try to locate him within our contemporary understanding of reality, the more we are in danger of restricting his activity to within the process as we know it. This could lead to a subjection of theology to a new and dangerous kind of cultural conditioning. Clearly God, if he is to be the Christian God, must be greater than our conceptions of him and must transcend the process even as he is involved in it; the Barthians have taught us that (and the Whiteheadian distinction between the "primordial" and "consequent" natures of God was an attempt to do justice to it). Yet, if we are to say anything relevant about God in this day and age, it may be necessary to take risks in our identification of him, to say "lo here" and "lo there", fully realizing that we might be belittling him, or making fools of ourselves, or both. For if what Teilhard called fundamental faith in the World proved unfounded—if the process as man experiences it proved to be more demonic than divine—our God-hypothesis would be invalidated, and we would have no Barthian "Wholly Other" to flee to.

This after all is the dilemma of contemporary apologetic. The Barthian God, to whom nothing makes any difference and whose existence cannot be disproven, seems to the world to make no difference to human existence—and is rejected as irrelevant. Any alternative way of thinking about God runs the risk of being proved wrong—as so many seem to have been proved wrong already.

But at least the faith of the process-theologians—faith in the God of an evolving world—does "earth" our theology in a way that the other traditions which we have examined fail to do. We have seen that excessive idealism and transcendentalism, whether overt (as in Barthianism) or concealed (as in secular theology) makes a mature and critical faith in progress hard to affirm—as did the naïve immanentism of the pre-Barthian liberals. The Process approach, in which man and God are both really involved in, and yet transcend, nature and society, may help us in our search for a critical and "dialectical" faith in both natural and social evolution and progress.

By dialectical I mean two things. First, evolution should not be viewed in a monistic way. Second, it should not be seen as straightforward or mono-directional, nor all simply positive in its effect.

First, evolution is not monistic. Much theological thought on the source of ultimate power in the universe has been bedevilled by "either-or"; either an omnipotent, manipulative deity in complete control, leaving little room for genuine freedom on man's part (the logical implication of much orthodox and neo-orthodox thinking); or an apparent vacation by God of his seat of power in order to give man responsible control (the answer of secular theology, married uneasily with high-sounding phrases about "what God is doing in the world" and the I-You partnership between God and man). Process theology, however, based as it is on ontology of relationships, finds no need to assert God's omnipotence in the often apparently despotic sense of "orthodox" theology; rather, in asserting his omni-relationship, omni-influence and omni-passibility, it seeks to give a metaphysical grounding to Bonhoeffer's insight that the power of God lies in his weakness and in the power of love which does not derogate from man's derived creativity. To speak of shared power in a mutual relationship does not, of course, *solve* the problem of divine and human power; but it may help to point to an alternative to the "oriental despot" image of God. Since creatures, as well as God, have a substantive contribution to make to evolution, the outcome is not predetermined, however strongly it may be guided by the influence of divine Love.

So far there may appear to be a resemblance between process theology and the Social Gospel in the understanding of God's role in the world and hence in the pattern of progress. But where (it will be recalled) the Social Gospellers were accused by their successors of making light of the rifts and discontinuities in the evolving cosmos, process theology emphasizes the complexity and often erratic nature of progress. When the creation that "groans and travails" is viewed not monistically but in its infinite variety, when it is seen how the needs and aims of creatures conflict and how this conflict is seemingly built into the universe, it is not

E

surprising that progress is seen as a situation of great flux, in which extreme developments are encountered more often than the calm but sterile *via media* of compromise and in which there are wrong turnings, losses and waste.

Nevertheless there is an overall direction, best discussed in the work of Teilhard de Chardin.[1] It is a movement from the formlessness of primal matter, through increasing complexity and ramification of new forms of life, to an ever higher and higher level of *community*.[2] True community—as distinct from mere static unity—is only possible between highly-developed, self-conscious individuals;[3] hence the process of ramification, of forming more and more clearly autonomous individuals, is an important aspect of evolution. (A cat is more of an individual than a tree or an insect; a man more so than a cat.) But this growth of individuals is not ultimate; it is the formation of community— a community constantly growing richer and more complex, constantly surpassing itself—which is the guiding principle of the process.

Up till now I have been speaking of evolution in very general terms and have doubtless seemed to imply (as Teilhard does) that biological insights could be applied to social development. Is this legitimate? Do we not need to take a warning from Social Darwinism and refuse to reduce human life to biological laws?

It will be recalled that Social Darwinism was based on a Naturalistic hypothesis (man is "just a part of nature") and on the individualistic doctrine of the survival of the fittest, which held that it was to everyone's benefit that the best men should win in the social rat-race. Thus in most cases Social Darwinism led to a dangerous marriage of the science of the time and the most brutal aspects of a *laissez-faire* society; and for that reason such socially

[1] See especially his works *The Phenomenon of Man* and *The Future of Man*. Though an independent thinker he has contributed much to the Process movement

[2] Teilhard expounds this "dialectic" between the ramification and individuation which Darwin so emphasized and the concentration and "reflexion" which produces a higher level of community in many to the essays in *The Future of Man*. His vision of "community" is based firmly on his scientific discoveries about the trend of evolution, and though there is indeed an element of intuition here (as we shall discuss further below), it is one which would seem to make the most sense of the data, not to be imposed upon them from without

[3] For an interesting discussion of this and its application to cultural change see M. M. Thomas, "Modernization of Traditional Societies and the Search for a New Cultural Ethos", in the *Ecumenical Review*, October 1966

conscious biologists as Huxley sought to drive a wedge between the laws of nature and the laws of society. We have seen, however, that these basic premises need to be qualified. "Mind" has evolved from "life"; man, though intimately related to the animals, is yet more than they; so we need not fear that this new approach will lead to a naturalistic reductionism. Moreover community, not individuality, is now seen as the ultimate good; a community in which no one can achieve "wholeness" alone, or at his neighbour's expense. In the attainment of this good, especially perhaps in certain aspects of the economic process and the meeting of the more elemental needs, individual striving, competition, and aggression[1] may have a functional role to play for the benefit of all, but at the more profoundly and uniquely human levels of community life it is more likely to be achieved by co-operation and mutual support. So the new application of evolutionary theory to society need not lead to a sanctioning of *laissez-faire* in any area of life; rather it seems to demand a dynamic tension between individual and communal enterprise. The new awareness of reality as a total, many-levelled process seems to demand such a relationship—one neither of over-simple identification nor of discontinuity—between biology and the social sciences, if the whole cosmos, with man at its centre, is to be understood in terms of process and progress.

Humanity itself, then, is evolving, not now biologically but socially, in a far from deterministic way (far less rigidly patterned than would be true at lower levels of being, even though there is an element of freedom there too). It is evolving, however, in a clear direction; towards a complex community-of-individuals. And of this, for the Christian, Christ—the one most fully in communion with God, with his neighbours, even with nature,[2]

---

[1] The debate started by the ethologist K. Lorenz's book *On Aggression* is worth following in this context. The basic thesis of Lorenz and his disciples—that man has an innate intra-specific aggressive instinct which he needs to learn to control and cannot "wish away"—has been challenged in A. Montagu (ed.), *Man and Aggression*, in which the general argument is that such aggression is culturally learned, not innate. Be this as it may, the debate has thrown much light on functionality and dysfunctionality of aggression, both in animals and man; there is probably a link between man's almost unique propensity to intra-specific conflict and his highly developed sense of individuality with all its creative and destructive consequences

[2] The so-called "nature-miracles" of the Gospels are, I believe, an attempt to express this relationship—man and nature working together instead of (as usually the case in a "fallen" state) in conflict

and most fully "integrated" in himself[1]—is the spearhead, the effective symbol within history, in whose life and power man can share through the sacramental life of the Church and so be enabled to work more effectively in the upbuilding of this community.

Process-theology, then, both makes it possible to affirm the *fact* of progress and gives us some guide to the *direction* of progress; but it does neither in a simplistic way. Some interpreters (including many on the Catholic Left) have seen process-theology as equalling the Social Gospel in *naïveté*; affirming a smooth, automatic progress with no conflicts, no call for sacrifice, no place for *r*evolution in an *e*volutionary system. I do not believe this is fair—even to Teilhard (tremendous optimist though he was) and certainly not to the disciples of Whitehead. In a pluralistic system, as I have suggested, nothing is automatic; there is conflict, challenge, real evil, waste and loss—no smooth ascent. Evolution is so complex that it involves within itself many revolutions— radical turnings in new directions, involving sacrifice and cost. A central theme in process-theology is that God, in some real sense, suffers; because he participates in a process where his creatures assert themselves in sinful as well as creative fashions, where everything does not "go his way". It is costly (if we may put it so) to be God; it is then also costly to seek to be on God's side. The Cross—conflict, struggle, bitterness and tragedy— looms over history as much for the process-theologians as for Niebuhr.

Daniel Day Williams' book *God's Grace and Man's Hope* is by far the best summary of the contribution of process-thought to our ideas about progress, based as it is on a contrast between the Process approach to this problem and those of both the Social Gospel and the Niebuhrian tradition. Williams pleads for a more consistent acknowledgement of the fact that God is both Creator (hence Lord of history, such that real progress according to his will is possible) and Redeemer (which implies that history needs a redemptive force, that progress is not straightforward or free from deep cost and tragedy). The Social Gospellers, he believes, neglected the need for redemption; Niebuhr and the neo-orthodox

---

[1] This is a central theme in current Christian involvement in the world of psychiatric medicine. See F. Lake, *Clinical Theology*; also F. W. Dillistone, *The Christian Understanding of the Atonement*, ch. 8

suffered from an inadequate theology of creation.[1] The secular theologians he does not discuss (the original edition of the book dates from 1949); one might however, following his lead, legitimately accuse them of having inadequate doctrines of both creation *and* redemption. Like the neo-orthodox before them they show a Barthian lack of interest in the world of "nature" and natural science, leading to a vague, inadequately founded theology of creation;[2] and their precarious optimism about man's creative powers, together with their lack of interest in the Church and the "means of grace", suggests a rather simplistic attitude to redemption as something that can be taken for granted.

Process-theology, however, as Williams shows, seeks to avoid both these errors. It reveals to us a world in evolution, with God involved at every point both to evoke and encourage the urge to creativity, and to correct its excesses and transform its disasters by the power of grace and love, which, though everywhere operative, is focused through Christ and his Church.

It is time to sum up what we have said about process-theology's contribution, and where it succeeds in avoiding the inadequacies of other traditions in Christian thought about progress. First, as to the *fact* of progress; process-theology bases on modern science its affirmation of an evolving universe, and through the eyes of faith (though never operating independently of the scientific evidence) it sees this evolution moving in a definite direction. Progress is not (as perhaps some secular theologians, if they thought about the matter, might say) a precarious quality of man alone in an otherwise static and deterministic universe; it is—dare we say?—built into the very nature of reality.

However—and here we move towards the problem of the *nature* and *direction* of progress—it is not automatic; it is not a simple straight-line movement; and it is not painless.

First, it is not automatic; least of all at the human level, where, as Teilhard says, "Evolution . . . charges itself with an evergrowing measure of freedom".[3] Every creature has the opportunity

[1] Williams, op. cit., ch. 1

[2] On the Barthian attitude to science cf. Barbour, op. cit., ch. 13 and *passim*. Whatever may be said about the "world-awareness" of secular theology, it can hardly be said that it shows more interest than neo-orthodoxy in building a new scientific world view and a new understanding of nature. Its radical division between "nature" and "history", stronger than Niebuhr's, and its obsession with the latter at the expense of the former, confirms this

[3] Teilhard de Chardin, *The Future of Man*, p. 72

to contribute to progress or to thwart it; and even the greatest optimist like Teilhard, whose faith in Christ as the "Omega" or goal of the universe creates a conviction that progress *will* go on, recognizes the possibility of an ultimate "opting out" of a whole section of the creation which refuses to co-operate in the achievement of the goal.[1] A degree of freedom for every creature is an essential assumption in this pluralistic metaphysic, rejecting as it does all deterministic world views in the name of new scientific insights. God may evoke progress; he does not compel it; hence his will may, at least in the short run, be thwarted; sin is real, and there is a cost of frustration to be borne in the ongoing march of progress.

Thus too evolution does not move in a straight line. Sometimes it involves "branching out"; ramification at the biological level, individual self-affirmation and creativity at the social level. Yet in this affirmation of selfhood, as well as the opportunity of enrichment, lies the fundamental risk of selfishness, separation from the community, sin and alienation; so that the trend towards individuality is ambivalent and needs periodic correction. And even were this not so, movement of the process to a higher level would still require the converse trend to what Teilhard calls "reflexion", the in-folding of the fruitful branches to form a new achievement of community and harmony of an ever richer and more complex kind. Thus progress means, now a movement of creativity and individuation such as the secular theologians extol; now a movement inwards towards greater and deeper community; which yet must in turn be challenged, lest it identify itself with *the* absolute Community, the Kingdom of God, and so become static and stultifying.

And all this is not painless. To move outward from static group security to individual adventure is risky; it may involve loss of one's fundamental being, especially in so far as this involves being-in-the-tribe; and while one may find oneself in this venture as an independent self, one may also lose one's selfhood as quickly as it is found. In the creative strivings of mankind there are genuinely wrong turnings and blind alleys. But the individualistic self-affirmation which this creativity evokes in turn makes the new establishment of a higher community of love very difficult; autonomous proud Self must suffer apparent loss to gain this,

[1] Teilhard de Chardin, *The Phenomenon of Man*, pp. 316f.

its true good. Conflict between individuals, and between the individual and a false and oppressive community, both cause real and seemingly inevitable evil within history.

So the *direction* of progress—this complex, costly struggle—is towards an ever richer life of community. Individual autonomy—that "freedom" of man from excessive dependence on the past, on the community, on nature, and on God—which secular thought so values, is not, and must not be preached as, the ultimate good, though it has its part to play in stimulating creativity and responsibility. A higher good must be held out before secular man; for we have already seen some of the results of his "pragmatic" world view, the points at which a Christian must say that it has proved a disastrous failure from the point of view of the increase of human well-being.

But what about the specific *guidance* which theology should give to Christians (and others) as they seek to know how to co-operate with this "progressive" God and his evolving creation? Here it must be said that, although process-theology contains hints towards a new ethical methodology, and although some valuable general reflections on social issues are found in Williams' book already mentioned, there has yet been no major contribution from this source towards the current discussions of Christian social ethics; and certainly the basic method of a Christian approach to the problems of society must be found, at best, at an implicit rather than explicit level in the writings of process-theologians.

What form might one expect a "Process social ethics" to take? It would be bound to pay great regard, more than traditional Christian ethics has ever done, to the witness of the natural and social sciences. It cannot divide "what is" and "what ought to be" as rigidly in its thought as Hume and the whole secular tradition has done. The "is", as revealed by empirical study, *points to* the "ought", as its "depth-dimensions" are seen by those who have vision. It is not of course identical with the ought; certainly not in the shallow sense that "all men ought to do what most men actually do", the doctrine that might well lead some to use, say, the Kinsey Report as a clear guide to sexual morality. The relationship between "is" and "ought" lies at a deeper level; that of the discovery of the "true nature of man". And this quest involves a subtle combination of pragmatism and idealism, of empirical study and religious or quasi-religious insight. Let me elucidate.

The process-theologian believes that, when we see reality-as-a-whole, it should become clear what man's real good is; there is no need to import from outside some transcendent norms ("you ought to do X") which are totally independent of the state of affairs that exists and derive their force either from their intrinsic worth or from the authority of their source (God, the conscience, or whatever). In this sense, process-ethics is pragmatic; it says, "You ought to do what *works*, what is functional for the total 'society of being'".[1] But this pragmatism is not only based on a much wider and deeper view of reality than the "instant pragmatism" of secular theology; it requires an element of *vision*. No one would assert, I think, that the Process view of reality can be read directly and unambiguously out of the discoveries of modern science; it views these discoveries *in a certain way*—what Wittgenstein described as "seeing-as", what Ramsey might call a "disclosure-situation",[2] and Dewey and Whitehead an aesthetic judgement.

The best example of this is Teilhard's own vision of a world in evolution towards a richer form of community. His scientific discoveries about the direction of evolution led him to visualize the world process as tending towards such a coming-together, a deeper oneness of all things, and to assert this both as the truest picture of the way things actually are, and as a foretaste of the ultimate goal—what should and will be. Teilhard is not a purely "objective" scientific thinker in the traditional sense, but neither is he a pure poet or mystic; the distinction between "objective" study and "subjective" evaluation has little relevance to his thought —and his critics, working on a more dualistic philosophy, usually fail to understand this.

When, by such an act of vision—a leap of faith which is yet grounded in the nature of things as science reveals it to us[3]— the world is seen in a certain way, there begins to emerge, I would

[1] This, roughly, is the kind of pragmatism for which John Dewey, William James, and C. S. Peirce stood. cf. Dewey, *Experience and Nature*, especially chs. 9–10, and other works.

[2] cf. I. T. Ramsey, *Religious Language*

[3] Science too, of course, forced as it now is to relinquish in certain areas its claim to "objectivity", may be regarded as a way of seeing-as; the scientist makes a quasi-aesthetic judgement in devising and testing his hypotheses and judging their appropriateness. cf. Barbour, op. cit., ch. 7

suggest, an understanding of what is "functional" for its well-being and enrichment, and hence an awareness of what men ought to do in order to contribute to this.[1]

It is in the controversial field of sexuality that the process-theologians have made their only real contribution to ethical thought so far.[2] I do not propose to discuss this, but only to point out that this is one area where, because of the profound element of "mystery" in interpersonal relationships, the secular kind of pragmatism has little to offer. It is noteworthy that Cox's discussion of sex[3] is extremely confused and that he is at times forced back on to most un-secular talk about "the *mysterium tremendum* of the sexual".[4]

By analogy it would seem that, in the field of social and political ethics, process-theology's most helpful contribution will be at those points where, as we have already seen, the secular approach has signally failed; the issues of race and poverty. In the next chapter, therefore, I propose to take up the theme of "development", with especial reference to the economic development of the Third World (now becoming such a major concern of the Churches), and to discuss some recent thinking which may well point the way forward, from a Process point of view, for future theological discussion on this and related issues.

[1] cf. Helen Oppenheimer's idea—very congenial to the Process emphasis on newness and creativity—that morality is an "art", a search to create a new and more aesthetically satisfying state of affairs with the materials to hand, as much as it is a "science" of conformity to existing laws. H. Oppenheimer, "Moral Choice and Divine Authority", in I. T. Ramsey (ed.), *Christian Ethics and Contemporary Philosophy*

[2] cf. especially the writings of W. N. Pittenger

[3] Cox, *The Secular City*, ch. 9   [4] ibid., p. 203

6

Progress and "Development"

It has, perhaps, been only in recent years that economic development has become a major concern of human life. Economic *survival*, of course, has always been an absolutely basic concern; but as long as development was not thought to be possible, as long as men held a static view of their social and economic order, survival alone was the aim of economic activity. Equally when development, the increase of wealth, began to be observable two or three centuries ago, the belief in "iron laws of economics" led men to assume that its path was more or less predetermined—and again the need to work for development was not a major concern.[1] Today, however, it is a live issue, both within and between nations. Why?

At the same time that the possibility of development has come to be taken for granted its automatic nature has ceased to be accepted. First, within the developed nations, the problem of trade cycles has had to be tackled by Keynesian fiscal policies; economic growth can and must be controlled if we are to avoid violent swings between inflation and recession. And the "revolution of rising expectations" leads people to expect such a controlled growth in their standard of living.

But as between nations the problem is more acute. As our world becomes smaller and its nations more interdependent it becomes ever more painfully obvious that some countries are less economically advanced than others, that the already rich are developing much faster than the still poor, and in some measure at their expense. More and more the people of the still poor countries—

[1] Of course many early economists such as Malthus were distinctly gloomy in their exposition of these "laws"; they held out no prospect of long-term improvement. But in any case, the changes they foresaw were all viewed deterministically. cf. A. K. Cairncross, *Factors in Economic Development*, ch. 1. A most valuable general introduction to the history of economic ideas is R. Heilbroner, *The Making of Economic Society*

however static the ideology and the economic system from which they are emerging—want development; and more and more the problems appear so massive as to demand a concerted international development effort on a world scale never known before.

The reasons why some countries have developed more rapidly than others are complex. Barbara Ward[1] attributes the differential primarily to ideological causes—the difference between the nations of the West, imbued with the Judaeo-Christian sense of the dynamic and purposive nature of history and the worthwhileness of the material order, and those of the East with their more static, and in many cases mystical and world-denying, outlook. There is some plausibility in this view; though we must also take into account other factors alongside, and probably influencing, the ideological ones, such as climatic difference, ratio between population and fertile land, and so on. Whatever the cause, however, one harsh fact obtrudes itself. The "late starters", seeking in our time to lift themselves above subsistence level, begin with a disadvantage; unlike those who colonized the Americas, they have little virgin soil to till, either literally or metaphorically. The already rich nations of the West loom over them as potential competitors in their every enterprise, especially where ·(as is agreed to be generally true, though it has been overemphasized in the recent past) development involves the expansion of a poor country's industrial sector and an attempt to break into rich markets with industrial products.

In order to complete this setting of the scene a brief mention of the effects of colonialism is necessary. Most of the poor countries, once European colonies, are geared to the production of raw materials for metropolitan markets. For various reasons the price which these materials can command tends to be unstable, and they can often be replaced more cheaply by man-made substitutes (or in the case of foodstuffs by the domestic production of such rich countries as the U.S.A.). Meanwhile the imports, of both capital and consumer goods, which the poor countries need in order to raise their standard of living tend to increase in price because of the inflationary trend within the rich countries which produce them. This leads to a situation of growing impoverishment, with imports more expensive and exports (at least since 1958) commanding less earning power every year.

[1] B. Ward, *The Rich Nations and the Poor Nations*

I have not mentioned either the problem of the imbalance in educational facilities (created to provide colonial clerks, not entrepreneurs or engineers) and the resultant critical lack of vital skills; or, what is perhaps the most notorious aspect of the whole problem, the population explosion. The magnitude of the crisis—twenty per cent of the world's population holding (roughly) eighty per cent of its wealth, and an increasing share at that, in a world which cries out for interdependence across the ever-widening gap between rich and poor—has been sufficiently sketched to show that the economic development of the Third World must be a vital area of moral concern at the present time.

For this reason, through national governments and inter-national bodies, "concerned" individuals and groups—not least, today, the Churches—have worked to make available unprece-dented (and yet, to date, all too small) resources to the poor nations to provide them with a vital proportion of the capital and the foreign exchange which they need in order to develop. Alongside this, though with perhaps less enthusiasm and even less success, has gone an effort to liberalize trade, tariff, and international monetary policies in the poor countries' favour. Over the last ten or fifteen years these concerns have resulted in an international effort of major dimensions.[1] But today momentum is showing signs of slowing down, not least because of a lack of political goodwill and support among the rich countries' electorates.

A cynic might ask how indeed it is politically possible for a government to give away any of its people's money. The answer is that aid has been given for a variety of reasons[2]—the currying of political favour, the buttressing of a friendly régime, the pro-tection of the donor country's investments in the area. Sometimes it has undoubtedly been given for purely humanitarian reasons; but one suspects that this proves politically easier in an emergency situation, such as famine, earthquake, or the aftermath of war, rather than for long-term development. Sometimes, perhaps, the need to build up a healthy, all-embracing world economy may have been at the back of the donors' minds; but this is such a long-term and speculative project that one doubts whether such "enlightened self-interest" has often prevailed over counsels of more immediate benefit to the donor.

[1] cf. I. M. D. Little and J. M. Clifford, *International Aid*, ch. 1
[2] Analysed in Little and Clifford, op. cit., ch. 3

To appeal to a rich country to give aid to a poor one simply so that the latter may develop its own economy—becoming then perhaps an importer from the donor country, but perhaps also or instead a competitor to it—may seem to be asking for a degree of altruism which (if Niebuhr was right) a nation, as distinct from individuals, does not and cannot possess. In the long run indeed it may be in everyone's interests that the poor countries should have a healthy and growing economy; but in the long run, as Lord Keynes reminded us, we are all dead. The "pragmatism" by which "secular men" and secular nations act cannot take the leap of faith which this long view entails; the long term is not controllable; it requires an act of vision to grasp its needs and opportunities, as the pursuit of short-term self-interest (enlightened or otherwise) does not. Only the visionary, he who has eyes to see, can affirm with conviction that in the long run man's real good lies in unreserved economic co-operation between nations.[1]

The difficulty of building an international development programme on a basis of secular pragmatism is only one of the current problems. Another is the degree of disillusionment among the electors of donor-countries when aid programmes "fail", or are received with less than humble gratitude, or are used to support a government whose standards of democracy are not those of Westminster. Many people seem to expect aid to be a panacea which, once pumped into a country, will automatically produce economic development—and any concomitant social and political problems will fall into place. And when the poor countries fail to reproduce in faithful detail (but without, of course, any of the generally acknowledged mistakes) the success story of the rich Western democracies, public opinion in the donor countries inevitably becomes cynical.

It is increasingly recognized that the problem here lies in an inadequate understanding of what development is. Many people are suggesting that the root of the trouble with the international aid programme today, lies in the reluctance to ask "What?" before asking "How?" Before we work out how to achieve economic development, we need to know more clearly what we are trying to achieve. The need for aid of the right "quality", allied to appropriate trade policies and so on, designed to achieve calculated and

[1] cf. above, pp. 65–6, for an exposition of this "pragmatism-in-depth" or "long-view pragmatism" as an ethical methodology

appropriate objectives, rather than money thrown around at random (or in a pattern dictated by considerations other than developmental) in the hope that it will do some good; this is a constant theme of the more informed critics of existing aid programmes.[1] But even before these demands can be met, we need to ask what the appropriate objectives are. What indeed *is* this ideal of "development" towards which we are supposed to be working? Merely an increase in the Gross National Product of a country? Or a subtle and complex process of change involving (as economic change inevitably does) questions of social justice, political superstructure, and the whole framework of culture and common life? It is in its inability to answer these questions, I would suggest, that a narrow pragmatism again shows its inadequacy; profound questions of value, of the meaning and destiny of human life, are at issue here.

What I am suggesting, then, is that the pragmatic approach to the question of overseas aid and development is beginning to look a little threadbare. It would appear that the rich Western nations are entering a period of isolationism, of disillusionment with their involvement in the wider world. The clearest signs of this perhaps are in the United States, where the gradual withdrawal from Vietnam and the "Nixon doctrine" of non-intervention in Asia and Africa have been accompanied by less desirable manifestations of isolationism, namely successive cutbacks in the overseas aid budget (which comprises almost half the world's total aid flow) and most recently a new policy of trade restrictions in the face of balance-of-payments difficulties. But indeed few nations have increased their aid, and many have not even maintained its real value, over the past few years. As far as trade is concerned, despite protectionist moves in some quarters, there seems to be a widespread acceptance of the principle of preferences for imports from the Third World; but it remains to be seen how much of this is mere lip-service, and in any case no really radical developments are likely in the present climate of public opinion. And the chronic instability in the world monetary system, the lifeblood of international trade, which has come to a head as I write, hits the developing nations harder than anybody—but their plight appears to be the last to be considered.

[1] cf. especially the annual Reviews of British aid policies, and other publications, of the Overseas Development Institutes

In so far as there has been progress it has probably been largely due to the insistent lobbying in many rich countries which has grown out of that minority public concern to which I referred earlier. It is significant that in this crusade the Churches have, for once, been in the forefront. The driving force of a wider vision and a deeper faith than secular ideology can offer is nowhere more evident than in the (perfectly understandable) situation of ambivalent and flagging public concern about the needs of the Third World.

There is, then, little reason for optimism that the rich countries will take their international responsibilities seriously on the basis of secular pragmatism. For, as I have already suggested, the basic motivation of Western aid has almost certainly been neither charity nor a concern for world development; the imperialistic impulse (however genuine the concern for the good of the world in which it was expressed), the desire to spread Western influence and the Western way of life as a bulwark against Communism, has probably been the principal driving force in the West, with an equivalent concern behind the Soviet aid programme. Niebuhr's few references to the aid programme in his later works see it as an example of the natural self-interest of nations being diverted along lines conducive to the general good.[1] Unfortunately, as we have seen, this period is now over; along with a diminution of concern for international power has gone a diminished awareness of international responsibilities. And this is a problem intractable in terms of the "realism" of Niebuhr and Cox. Has the new Christian socialism, and the process-theology which (I believe) provides its necessary metaphysical foundation, anything to contribute at this critical juncture?

A possible answer to this question may be found by an examination of the prevailing "ethos" of development and an analysis of its shortcomings. Two of the most significant Christian books on development—Richard Dickinson's 1968 study for the World Council of Churches, *Line and Plummet*, and Charles Elliott's more recent *The Development Debate*—are both largely (the first almost entirely) devoted to such an analysis, and what follows draws heavily on them.

Dickinson defines the prevailing philosophy of development,

[1] cf. Niebuhr, *The Structure of Nations and Empires*, for a study of the dynamics of the new imperialisms of Washington and Moscow

current among the majority of those involved in rich and poor countries alike, as fundamentally rationalist. It reflects an over-concern with economic "expansion" at the expense of social "growth";[1] a preference for investing in potential "success" projects (and whole nations) rather than helping those with less potential; and an interest in "structures" rather than "people". In short, it reflects some of the weaknesses we have observed in the current secular ideology, where economic and pragmatic criteria are in danger of taking the place of a search for more profound objectives as guides for decision-making.

Before I discuss some of the hints that this sort of analysis gives towards the need for a new philosophy and theology of development I must enter a fundamental caveat. Some Christians (and other men of ideals) may, as Dickinson notes,[2] be repelled not only by the basic pragmatic premises of the "development ethos" but by the techniques used in economic planning. It is sometimes claimed that the use of any economic criteria (of cost-benefit analysis in particular) to determine the direction of social change is itself demonic. "Economic" and "human" criteria are regarded as mutually exclusive, and the "dismal science" thereby becomes a modern scapegoat devoted to the new Azazel, the Demon of the Asphalt Jungle.

I do not believe that an incarnational theology can permit this writing-off of a whole area of human endeavour. The "theology of cost-benefit analysis" has been too little considered, but such a theology there must be. Briefly, cost-benefit analysis investigates how to make the best possible use of scarce resources in the attainment of chosen objectives. It is a refinement, and a most welcome one, of traditional economic techniques in the emphasis it places on the "objectives" side of the question. There is certainly a theology of resources (based on the ideas of creation and stewardship), and surely also, as we shall see, a theology of objectives. Thus the relationship between the two is a rightful concern for the thinking Christian. The danger (for of course this tool is not value-free) is that both costs and benefits may be interpreted too narrowly, and that the complex needs of human beings, and the sacrifices they must make in order to satisfy these needs,

---

[1] For a good discussion and concrete application of these two concepts in the Third World cf. L. Barnes, *African Renaissance*
[2] Dickinson, op. cit., p. 35

may be reduced to the economic factors which are easiest to quantify. This only emphasizes the need for careful analysis on the political, sociological, and theological levels of the human dimensions of the equation.

What then *are* the rightful goals of development, and what are the evaluative factors that must be borne in mind in the quest for these goals? They are summed up in most contemporary theological thought by an emphasis on the category of "the Human" (*humanum*) which is the subject of an ongoing World Council study at the present time.

What does this rather vague-sounding ideal mean? It is generally set against any economic or socio-political considerations which narrow down our understanding of man in his complexity. Hence any attempt to take non-economic factors into account in development thinking is certainly to be welcomed as a step towards making "humanization" possible. Elliott[1] instances the United Nations' use, in the past few years, of a tentative scale of "social indicators" (health, nutrition, consumption of basic goods, and so on); the increasing emphasis among economists on the place of structural change in economic growth; and finally the concern with the political aspect of development, leading to an emphasis on social justice and power for the oppressed summed up in the term "liberation". But all these—even the last—may, he suggests, take insufficient account of certain aspects of human need. For "humanization" implies more than greater wealth, greater efficiency, even greater economic and social justice. In the words of *Populorum Progressio*, Pope Paul VI's notable Encyclical on development, it means "to have more in order to *be* more". To the proponents of "humanism" in the developing nations (notably Presidents Kaunda of Zambia and Nyerere of Tanzania) it includes the building of genuine community and solidarity on the foundation of African tradition, and the realization of moral and spiritual values, within a context of economic growth, social justice and a sense of national identity and self-reliance.

Thus although humanization may seem a rather ill-defined concept it can be used as a vehicle for certain important and positive emphases. What needs to be developed further at this stage perhaps is a better definition of what humanization is *not*. This may lead us to a clearer understanding of why such a concept is

[1] Elliott, op. cit., chs. 3–5

F

necessary, which in turn will point to needed areas of more precise definition. And from there we can go on to look for some indication of the resources, theological and sociological, on which we might draw to give the idea still more positive content.

We have already seen, in part, what humanization is not. It is not what Elliott calls developmentism; rather it attempts to transcend this narrow concern with economic growth and other over-simplifications of the development ideal. I repeat this because its theological implications are so vital. For it seems to me implicit that the ideal of humanization (despite its use by some secular theologians such as Paul Lehmann) must base itself, philosophically and theologically, on something more profound than secular pragmatism.

This is increasingly recognized. In the recent symposium by the Humanum Foundation, *Technology and Social Justice*, theologians of many different traditions repeatedly criticize secular theology[1] and, whilst clearly recognizing its positive value in broadening our understanding of God's work in the world and of the nature of Christian social concern, show that it is an insufficient basis for theological thought about "humanization". For the nature and destiny of man is a metaphysical question, and (as we shall see) an understanding of man in his wholeness must consider a number of areas of human experience which the secular theologians do not adequately consider.

And this, of course, is why such an understanding is so sorely needed. Two new crises have manifested themselves on a more or less world-wide scale in the past few years, to which secular theology is likely to have even less to say than it does to the issues of race and poverty. One is the need for "roots" of a spiritual or quasi-spiritual type; the other, the problem of ecology, of man's place in nature.

The first crisis is observable in a number of forms. The search for identity in emergent nations, to which we have referred, is one; and whilst African leaders[2] have been to the fore in expounding this concern, it is perhaps the Indian theologian M. M. Thomas

[1] See especially the essay by Nash on ecology, and his long footnote 12 on p. 339 criticizing secular theology. The essays by Parmar and Nissiotis are also particularly relevant

[2] The concept of *Negritude*, emphasized by President Senghor of Senegal, should be mentioned here alongside Kaunda's Zambian Humanism and Nyerere's African Socialism

who speaks most effectively to Christians. Much of his work deals
with the need for a renascent India to find "spiritual foundations"
more appropriate to her contemporary situation than traditional
Hinduism, Anglo-Indian culture, or the more pietistic forms of
Christianity.[1] Thomas was one of the first to suggest that the
revolution in the Third World was forcing ancient, static religions
and cultures into a new awareness of the "personal" nature of
human existence, of the dynamic tension between individuality
and community and of the reality of history, which demands the
renewal of understanding—not the abandonment—of the classic
symbols of self-understanding in those cultures and religions.
His deep awareness that man (and supremely Third World
man) is a religious, cultural and symbolizing animal, not just a
political and economic one, has greatly influenced the present
writer and has played a large part in recent ecumenical debate.

But alongside this quest for identity in the new nations, we are
now seeing in Western society the phenomenon of radical alienation
from the prevailing, seemingly rootless culture; new forms of life
style, experiments with drugs and with Eastern religions, a restless
search for the spiritual roots which a secularized "Christian"
culture seems unable to provide.

Closely linked with this, in the minds of an increasing number of
young people in particular, is the second crisis: the problem of
ecology. Beginning from a concern with the threat of massive
environmental pollution, especially (but not only) in the
"developed" countries, the questioning has moved on to a more
fundamental plane. What is man's true relationship to nature?
Has the traditional Judaeo-Christian emphasis on his mastery
over nature (so emphasized by Harvey Cox) led to the kind of
exploitation which seems to be ruining our environment and could
spell the death of earth? How can we learn to see man-and-nature
as a whole, a "total process"? Does this require giving up our
obsession with economic growth and technological development?

Until very recently these were regarded as the questionings of
cranks. It is still often said (not always without justification) that
much concern with ecology is a luxury of the rich, who wish to
preserve their wide open spaces and can afford to put a low
priority on further economic growth. But scientists, politicians,
and spiritual questers alike are beginning to baulk at the dangers

[1] See especially his *The Christian Response to the Asian Revolution*, ch. 3

F*

of an irresponsible attitude to the environment, and some are speaking of an inevitable doom for the human race—either a continuation of growth policies leading to the death of earth through consequent pollution, or a halt to growth leading to economic stagnation and perhaps the starvation of half mankind.

We cannot effectively answer these prophets of doom until scientists and philosophers (and theologians) together have developed a more profound understanding of the interrelationship of the various parts of the natural order (including man) and the way in which ecological equilibrium may be achieved for the benefit (material and spiritual) of man and the health of his environment. Science alone cannot achieve such an understanding; for (as we saw in the previous chapter when we discussed Teilhard) science can only make sense of the world as a whole if backed by a metaphysic, a particular way of "seeing-as". And if the philosophers are necessary partners in the task of establishing a foundation for understanding ecology, how much more indispensable is their contribution to the formation of the human conscience and eliciting the human will to respond to this challenge.

Serious discussion of ecology on this kind of level (as distinct from impassioned cries to take it seriously) is only just beginning. Nash's essay in *Technology and Social Justice*, already mentioned, provides a useful short background note from a Christian viewpoint, and there are others. But the debate is still at an early stage, and where it will lead we cannot yet tell. Suffice it to say that a Christian voice is beginning to be raised in protest against the secular ideology that man is the master of nature without dependence on it or obligations to it; and that such a protest is increasingly based on what Nash[1] calls a "synoptic" theology, one which sees the wholeness of things and is not afraid of wrestling with the fundamental metaphysical issues raised by modern science.

However, there are dangers in these encouraging new moves to understand the wholeness of man. The "enlightened" response to the spiritual and ecological crises could easily lead to a new flight to the womb. Over-emphasis on man's inwardness and passivity and his dependence on nature could tempt men to escape that peculiarly human responsibility for action and change, that creative drive, which the secular theologians for all their faults rightly emphasized. And in the most unlikely places we could

[1] op. cit., p. 327

see the emergence of a dangerous neo-romanticism akin to what Niebuhr called the fundamental sin of Sensuality and Cox that of Sloth.

Clearly the relationship between man, society, and nature is more complex than either the secularizers and developmentalists, or the hippies and conservationists, recognize. Clearly Niebuhr's shrewd analysis of man's complexity, for all the somewhat abstract approach of which we accused him, is still very relevant. But rather than think—as he tended to do—about the nature and destiny of man *qua* individual, we must look at the nature of that "community of being" which binds the individual to society and man to nature.

Now that we have, perhaps, a better idea of the critical questions posed to those who seek a criterion of the Human today, how can we give this criterion some positive content? What is our source material? I have already suggested in the previous chapter that both theological and sociological factors, reacting upon each other, must enter into any adequate understanding of progress, of man's nature and destiny. Some of the issues raised by the social and natural sciences I have already glanced at and more will arise in the course of our discussion. We must now look more closely at the theological side.

Clearly, for Christians, the primary criterion of the human is Jesus, the Son of Man, *the* Man. In Teilhard's words, he is the Omega, the type and goal of what man is to become. The question immediately arises, what sort of man was—or is—Jesus? In the present state of confusion in both New Testament criticism and fundamental doctrine, what affirmations can we make about this strange figure?

One way of summing up the image presented to us in the Gospels is in the concept of reconciliation. The life and teaching of Jesus alike reveal a conviction that our world is a world of relationships in which man and God, man and man (and even in a sense man and nature) need to establish that combination of mutual obligation and mutual freedom which the Old Testament tradition called Covenant.[1] Such relationships, in their essence

[1] For three perspectives on the significance of the covenant idea in the contemporary situation see B. E. Meland, *The Realities of Faith*, ch. 2; J. M. Gustafson, "A Theology of Christian Community?" in E. de Vries (ed.) *Man in Community*; and C. C. West, "Status Quo, Evolution or Revolution?", in R. H. Preston (ed.), *Technology and Social Justice*

fragile, tend to distortion; and any attempt to shore them up by bonds of Law, whilst of some limited value and often necessary, in the long run replaces personal values by impersonal, judgemental relationships. The only way in which the destructive tension inherent in this situation can be made creative is through the offer of perfect, unconditional, unreserved love; such love alone can heal, and such love is the characteristic of Jesus. He is the one who accepts in himself the divisions and wounds of man and of the cosmos, and who in his life, death, and resurrection exemplifies in himself (and achieves for others) a costly communion with God, with other men, with nature, and with the very inner self which in ordinary men is so split and torn. Jesus thus is Reconciled and Reconciling Man—not simply "at one" in a static way with God and his neighbour, but in communion with them across the real divisions, the creative and destructive tensions, of the covenant relationship. In his life we see an image of what man in community might be. And this is more directly applied to the human situation through the concept of the Church as the Body of Christ, the ideal human community in which barriers are broken down, and each belongs to all and all to each.

The much misused and misunderstood doctrine of justification by grace accepted through faith is a codification of the Christian's experience of Christ and his Church which focuses our attention upon the inadequacies of many of the categories by which men order their common life. The demands of Law, the idealization of Merit, and the concomitant tensions of Guilt are all shown up for what they are—necessary evils at the very best, and at worst hindrances to "the glorious liberty of the children of God". This gives us some clue as to what is, and what is not, the kind of life in community which is acceptable to Christians. It implies, for example, that we should not, in a truly Christian world, lavish our praise or rewards (or our financial help) on the so-called deserving or successful,[1] and that relationships (including aid relationships) motivated by guilt can never be redemp-

---

[1] A central concern, it will be recalled, of both Dickinson and Elliott. As I have already pointed out, this does not invalidate the use of cost-benefit analysis to decide where aid, for example, can be most "successfully" used. The Christian simply has a more holistic criterion of success—what builds a true human community? what promotes equality, fellowship, and mutual responsibility?— than his secular counterpart, for whom the criterion of success will often be the return on a discrete investment to a particular nation or group

tive.[1] One may need to employ a certain realism about the possibility of turning the world—at every level from the family to international relations—into a covenant community; and as Niebuhr pointed out, the higher the level at which you are working, the less easy it is to put these ideals into practice. But they are part of the challenge with which Jesus presents the world, and his followers must reflect this as far as may be both in word and deed.

This very sketchy summary of some of the resources for theological consideration of the Human lead however to an acute paradox; one which, for the Christian, must be at the heart of his thinking about development. David Jenkins defines it as a belief in "the power of the powerless",[2] and Charles Elliott extends the *Populorum Progressio* definition of humanization to read "having more in order to be more—*in order to be less.*"[3] Self-fulfilment is found through self-giving, not (ultimately, however valuable a role it can sometimes play) through self-assertion;[4] for though man's "independence" has a creative value, he was made for *inter*-dependence with God, his neighbour and the cosmos. And the scars which cut across the network of relationships that is our world, run so deep that, for the Christian as for his Lord, "power" is not sufficient to heal them—only suffering love, perfect and utter self-giving. For this reason, the enhancement of material power, however necessary in given situations, can never be absolutized as the ultimate end of development; and equally, any entry of the Church into power politics will be fraught with ambiguities and risks.

But the Church must certainly identify herself, as did her Lord, with the dispossessed of the world, and especially with those "marginal men" who in rapidly changing societies are excluded equally from the sphere of traditional stability and the sphere of modern prosperity, and who are the prime casualties of the world economic process.[5] The form this identification will take must be whatever is the most effective for our time; a slavish

---

[1] cf. Lester Pearson, *The Crisis of Development*, p. 60

[2] Paper given to a consultation on the theology of development held by the WCC–Roman Catholic Commission on Society, Development, and Peace (SODEPAX) in November 1969

[3] Elliott, op. cit., ch. 9

[4] For an application of this to Western industrial man see my essay "Self-actualization and the Christian doctrine of work", *Church Quarterly*, January 1970

[5] Elliott, op. cit., ch. 5

following of the way in which our fathers in the faith, or Christ himself, attempted this identification, would be inappropriate. But it must bear the marks of suffering love, not mere power. The quest for a true world community, in which all men together can achieve their full stature as equal members of one body, requires that Christians sacrifice themselves as spokesmen and protagonists of the excluded ones.

Where then—and this has now become one of the most crucial questions in regard to the Church and development—do Christians stand on the issue of violent revolution? For it is, in general, the marginal men who are involved in the revolutionary movements of the Third World. There are many situations where a violent overthrow of the existing order seems to provide the only hope for any measure of justive and truly human life for these people. Can Christians share in violence, even against a violent and repressive establishment, for the sake of attaining justice? Can this end justify such means?

In principle it would seem not. Jesus rejected the philosophy of the Zealots in what some would claim was a similar "colonial" situation and chose a more excellent way to redeem the marginal men of Israel. Revolution is never the ultimate answer to the problem of injustice and alienation; and Christians must be very wary of it. Yet it may be the right way in a given situation and there may be cases where it would be wrong for Christians to opt out. This pressing problem may be discussed from two angles; the classical question of whether the end ever justifies the means, and the question, already raised implicitly in several contexts, of the relationship between conflict and reconciliation.

Two quotations from the controversial American community organizer, Saul Alinsky (a man, perhaps not well known outside the U.S.A., whose work in the slums and ghettoes has challenged and divided the American Churches as deeply as Vietnam) show clearly the related nature of these two questions. His favourite aphorisms, replete with the sardonic wit of the American Jew, are "Those who worry about the relationship of ends and means usually finish up on their ends without any means", and "Reconciliation usually means that one party gets all the power and the other party gets reconciled to it."[1] In short—as Niebuhr learned

[1] The issues raised by the work of Alinsky and others among the marginal citizens of the United States are well discussed from a Christian viewpoint

the hard way and taught so clearly—a perfectionist approach to the quest for social justice can obstruct that quest and be used to buttress the *status quo*—and Christians have perhaps too often been guilty of this.

One element in a Christian consideration of the possibility of a just revolution, it has been suggested, is the classical doctrine of the just war. This was based on the major premise that ends could sometimes justify means, and that the cost in terms of deaths and injuries, the brutalization of the participants and the disruption of society were sometimes worthwhile for the benefit of release from an intolerable situation of injustice. If this can apply to a war between states it can presumably apply to a war between groups within a state.

But of course the situation is complicated by the traditional Christian attitude towards the "powers that be". From St Paul's defence of the claims of citizenship in Romans 13, down through the ages, the mainstream tradition of Christianity has tended to place a high value on social order and on the rights of duly constituted authorities. This should not be sneered at by would-be radicals; the value of order in a sinful and hence fragile society is indeed great. But there are times, as some theologians in all traditions have been aware, when other values take precedence. Romans 13 stands to remind us of the moral risk and the social cost inherent in revolution; it should not be read as a rigid commandment never to participate in it.

This does mean however that violence must be quite clearly recognized as the inherent evil that it is. A revolution can only be redeemed—since like all human activities it is in need of redemption—if at all times, however paradoxical it may sound, the participants act in a spirit of reconciliation.

For I hope it will already have become clear that conflict and reconciliation are not—indeed cannot and must not be—mutually exclusive. The achievement of reconciliation, of justice and love, often requires conflict—if only the conflict of words between Jesus and the Pharisees, or the imprecations of the prophetic witness, which must continue to set the normative pattern for Christian activity in the quest for justice. Any human relationship, even a marriage, which is free from tension and conflict is a lifeless

by L. E. Schaller, *Community Organization: Conflict and Reconciliation*, to which this discussion is indebted.

thing. Conflict is endemic in a pluralistic and sin-ridden society of being. And there are times when the conflict that lies below the surface in an alienated situation must be brought to the surface, and the paper that covers the cracks must be torn away.

The ultimate moral question is whether those who engage in such conflict are ready to bear the cost of it in their own bodies— as some Christians such as Camillo Torres certainly have been. This may seem a strange *via crucis*; but may it not have redemptive and reconciliatory power?

Equally, however, conflict in the name of justice requires a constant effort at reconciliation. As the title of a propagandist publication a few years ago reminded us, "white South Africans are *also* people". Can the Christian revolutionary love his enemy— or rather the enemy of Christ's poor—and seek to redeem him, even if, at the end of the day as the (humble) instrument of God's justice, he is forced to shoot him? This is the intolerable demand laid upon the Christian who chooses the guerrilla's way; and it differs only in degree from that faced by the Christian community organizer or even the Christian trade unionist. And in such a situation we must remember that we are saved by grace, not works, and may be called upon to sacrifice even our "righteousness" for the cause of Christ's poor.

The question of revolution, then, remains open. As such it illustrates the "intolerable shirt of flame" which the Christian concerned about development is called upon to wear. It is only as we offer ourselves unconditionally in the service of humanity, knowing that we will be "consumed by either fire or fire", that we can take part in the redemption of God's world—that redemption for which, torn by revolution, pollution, and all the other shatterers of "developmentist" optimism, the world groans and travails.

It will by now be clear that this appeal to the criterion of the Human in our thinking about development poses questions rather than provides answers. If anything it makes the questions more poignant and painful. But it provides a few positive hints for our theological analysis of the problems which face our evolving world. It reminds us, first, that our idea of human community must be nothing less than universal, and that it must be characterized by reconciliation and love rather than by individualism or collectivism. Such a community (which in a sense stretches beyond the boundaries of mankind to include nature too) can only be achieved by drawing out men's deepest aspirations, their longing for spiritual foundations, and focussing them on a goal greater than even that of the community itself. A new argument for the existence of God (or rather, a new way of questioning those who ask the question about God, and pointing them towards the possibility and necessity of God) might profitably be based upon this need for a truly universal and infinite focus of human aspiration which will draw the community of being above and beyond itself.[1] And in the present critical situation (whatever the secularizers may say) God is "needed" more than ever, though our faith in him may be somewhat different in detail, and in some ways more agnostic, than has been true of our forebears.

Secondly, our discussion of the Human has led us to an emphasis on the power of the powerless, the significance of suffering in the process of redemption, which has always of course been central in Christian faith but has rarely been adequately spelt out in terms of social ethics. This in turn leads us to a new awareness of the need for a transvaluation of the world values of power and success, even whilst these values are accorded a limited utility. And hence it reminds us that man's need and God's gift is always greater than the designs and ideologies devised by men, and that they must all come under the judgement of the Cross.

These hints which I have developed above can hardly be called a complete Christian theology of development (if indeed such an enterprise be possible). Nor have I given much in the way of practical guidelines for Christian participation in the development struggle. What I have sought to show is the way in which this new, almost apocalyptic, aspect of mankind's quest for the more abundant life has challenged to its very roots the more naïve Christian and secular approaches to progress. In such a situation the response of the secular theologians is particularly inadequate. If the world alone sets the agenda the meeting will dissolve in chaos. And, as we have seen, many theological critics are beginning to recognize the need for a vision and a hope, of man in community with God, his neighbour, nature, and his inner self, which will energize the Church (and through it, others) to new levels of

[1] This is being worked out by, among others, the American Jesuit philosopher Robert Johann whose collection of essays *Building the Human* has recently been published in this country

action—and suffering—on behalf of God's groaning and travailing world.

What this will mean in practice cannot be laid down for all situations. The challenge of development is indeed global; but in different countries, and to different individuals and groups, the challenge will present itself in perhaps dramatically different ways. But one thing is certain. While we must avoid a definition of development so wide as to include the whole onward march of human history—and so rob it of substantive meaning—we must realize that economic growth in one country or group of countries cannot be examined in isolation from the growth of political justice, social community, the husbandry of natural resources, and indeed spiritual enlightenment, within and amongst all nations.

The Christian, then, must criticize every development within any society which fails to do justice to the image of man that we see in Christ: the "whole man" in community, under God, not conforming to some static ideal but making himself and discovering himself in the dynamic and costly process of conflict and reconciliation which is the very law of life. He must hold the foundation of this vision, as revealed in Bible and Church, in creative tension with those hard social realities which shape the pattern of human striving. The Christian, of all men, if his faith is valid, can most afford to be free from blinkers; he can face the hard facts of economic and political reality without allowing them to destroy his vision. For it is in the flesh of the Christian administrator, campaigner—or perhaps guerilla—that the tensions between the ideals of Christ and the "reality" of the present age, between apparently incompatible ideals, between the quest for reconciliation and the necessity of conflict, are themselves reconciled. And so ultimately Jenkins and Elliott are right. Whatever its form may take in particular circumstances, the Christian concern for "development" must be the political outworking of a cruciform spirituality.

7

Conclusion

We return, then, after our wanderings down so many pathways, to the question with which we began. Can Christians affirm faith in human progress?

We have seen how the Social Gospellers attempted to do so—and failed through lack of realism, through their naïve imaginings of a growing harmony in society and their failure (largely culturally conditioned) to recognize the rifts and conflicts endemic in all life. We have seen how the Barthians, shaking themselves free (as they thought) from such cultural entanglement, in effect withdrew God from the world, leaving their successors to affirm "secularity" and "freedom" as the emerging destiny of man on earth. We have seen how Niebuhr in particular, still the giant of our century among theologians of society, failed through his very emphasis on "realism" to solve the problems raised by the Social Gospellers, and prepared the way for that strange amalgam of utopianism and iconoclasm, of religious pessimism and secular pride, which characterized most American (and so much other) theology during the last decade. Finally we have seen how the process-theologians have sought a new understanding of the relationship of God to the world, and the Catholic Left a parallel understanding of the life of man in community, in the face of the growing threat to secular optimism posed with especial poignancy by the crisis of the Third World.

Today more than ever man needs a faith; for "things fall apart, the centre cannot hold", at the very time when the growing and fragile interdependence of man and man, man and nature, needs a "centre" to maintain it. If the Christian Gospel is true, the only possible centre in the last analysis is the God manifested in Jesus of Nazareth and pointed to and served (however inadequately) by the Church in and through which he lives. Perhaps, as we face the contemporary crisis, we can at least proceed along a kind of *via negativa* in order to discover what the Christian faith for today must *not* be; only by continual questing, individually and together, can we discover (imperfectly and provisionally) what it *is*.

It cannot, I would suggest, be a faith in an unchanging God transcendent above the flow of time and calling men into a Kingdom the ideal of which is a static community. The faith of the charlady who intended in Heaven "to do nothing for ever and ever" is not a faith for our frenetic times and, if we have something to learn from our less activist forefathers in this respect (as the spiritually hungry young are reminding us), we do well to remember that Christ's peace is not the peace which the world gives; not peace above the flux, but the peace of finding the pattern of his will within the flux. If this is to be so of us, how much more so of God himself. The "Unmoved Mover" of classical theism, and the concomitant metaphysic, cannot serve as valid Christian symbols in the face of the genuine discoveries of contemporary man about the dynamic, conflict-ridden nature of society, the cosmos, and himself. The Christian God is more "living" and involved than even the secular theologians, with all their emphasis on the God of History, can ever acknowledge.

Equally, a faith for our times cannot be directed to a God who leaves the world to work out its own salvation in a quest for "secularity" and "freedom" in which restless conflict is at a premium and community and spirituality are at a discount. This is the other side of the coin of our discovery of the livingness of God and the primacy of relationships. The secular theologians have directed our gaze to the "this-worldly" emphasis in our faith and the danger of quasi-theocracies and of the idolatry of "togetherness"; but in so doing they have all but idolized the pragmatic, individualistic society of the contemporary west. Some of us, at least, have not so learned Christ.

The new left Catholicism, and the theology of process, have their evident dangers. They too could lead to a too easy accommodation between Christianity and certain elements in contemporary culture (though these, I would maintain, are the most creative and dynamic elements). They too could lead to a social and metaphysical monism—or equally easily, to a dissolution of God in the flux of time or an idolatry of permanent revolution. Yet they do attempt, in a way which the other traditions which we have examined fail to do, to come to terms with some of the crises facing modern man.

First, as we have seen, they seek to do justice to the dialectical nature of life and of all reality. In doing so they are able to relate the classical philosophical tension between the One and the Many with the discoveries of the natural and social sciences about the evolution of individuation and the quest for community. Whilst their exploration of these themes at the sub-human level (I refer of course primarily to Teilhard's work) are highly speculative, they may serve to help us see the universe as a whole and to make some sense of the complexity of the evolutionary process. At the human and social level this relevance is clearer. We have only just begun to wrestle with a theological approach to the nature of community and the place of conflict within it as presented to us by the social scientists. But clearly the picture is more complex than the ideology of secularity would have us believe.

The new theological thinking also attempts to come to terms with the spiritual heart-searchings of modern man as well as his political and economic problems. It implies that our secular culture, if it is to meet man's deepest needs, requires a new "sacralization" to make man aware of his place in the great society of being and motivate him to participatory community living.[1] This leads to a renewed emphasis on the role of the Church and its sacramental life; for it is (or should be) supremely in the Eucharist that man's true nature in community through Christ is revealed. Worship and Christian community is not merely—as some would say—a possible means to an end, a motivating force for our involvement in secular progress; it is itself a locus of progress. For wherever Christians—in however broken and distorted a way —seek communion with God in prayer, with each other in fellowship and with both, focally, in the Eucharist, there a new step towards the Kingdom is taken, at least potentially and in germ. Something of this must surely happen too in other religions and in "purely secular" experiences of community; but it is particularly necessary at the present time that we should reaffirm, absurd as it may seem, the Body of Christ as the centre and vanguard of an evolving creation.

Finally, the new theologies at which we have been looking seek to relate these fundamental doctrines to the hard fact of the continued crucifixion of Christ in the bodies of his poor. Enough

[1] cf. Panikkar, "The People of God and the Cities of Man", in S. Verney (ed.), *People and Cities Conference Coventry '68*

has been said on this subject; it is the touchstone of an authentic theology for our generation, in so far as it challenges the implicit objectives of our contemporary culture and submits them to the judgement of the Cross.

Such, then, is the stage we have reached in our quest after the Christian meaning of human progress. And the quest must go on. We need to learn more about conflict and community in both "developed" and "developing" countries. We need to learn—the hard way—what reconciliation means in a torn and bleeding world. We need to learn the implications of a revolutionary spirituality based on the new vistas of meaning and possibility opened up to us by the natural, social, and psychological sciences and the lineaments of Christ which they show us. And we need to learn from history—the history of Christ in his Church, the history of our one divided world, and the history of that theological enterprise which has sought to relate the two. It is my hope that this brief exposition of recent theological trends will at least help Christians to embark on this latter investigation, and perhaps provide a foundation for thinking about some of the other, more fundamental, questions about the right Christian understanding of progress.

Index

Teilhard de Chardin, Pierre, 60–4, 66, 79, 89
Thomas, M. M., 60n, 76–7
Tillich, Paul, 10

van Buren, Paul, 36
van Leeuwen, Arend, 28, 29n
Vietnam, 27, 41, 72

Ward, Barbara, 69
Weber, Max, 31–2, 34n
"welfare capitalism", 39
West, Charles C., 11n, 17n, 19, 79n
Whitehead, A. N., 29n, 34n, 54, 56–7, 66
Wicker, Brian, 31n, 46–50
Williams, Daniel D., 6, 36n, 62–3
Winter, Gibson, 32n, 48n